EARLY NATURE ARTISTS *in* FLORIDA

Audubon and His Fellow Explorers

CHRIS FASOLINO

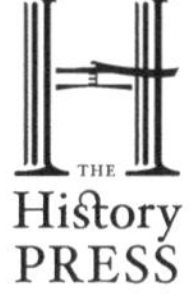

Published by The History Press
Charleston, SC
www.historypress.com

Front cover, top, left to right: Barred Owl by John James Audubon. *Digital image created by Oppenheimer Editions. Collection of the New-York Historical Society.* Parrotfish by Mark Catesby. *Courtesy of the Wilson Library, University of North Carolina, Chapel Hill.* Franklin Tree by William Bartram. *Courtesy of the American Philosophical Society. Front cover, main image*: Little Blue Heron by John James Audubon. *Digital image created by Oppenheimer Editions. Collection of the New-York Historical Society. Back cover*: Roseate Spoonbill by John James Audubon. *Digital image created by Oppenheimer Editions. Collection of the New-York Historical Society.*

First published 2021

Manufactured in the United States

ISBN 9781467150323

Library of Congress Control Number: 2021941040

Notice: The information in this book is true and complete to the best of our knowledge. It is offered without guarantee on the part of the author or The History Press. The author and The History Press disclaim all liability in connection with the use of this book.

For Mr. Pete,
with the love and appreciation
of his nephew Seadog

And for David Douglas,
a treasured friend, a true artist
and a future New World explorer

CONTENTS

INTRODUCTION

Increasingly amazed." That was how John James Audubon described his reaction to the natural wonders of Florida. As an artist, Audubon would become renowned for his brilliant and colorful portrayals of birds; thus, he found much to inspire him on his Floridian expeditions. From the elegance, grace and family loyalty of sandhill cranes to the aerial acrobatics and amazing migrations of terns to the endearing and comical appearance of pelicans, Florida's bird life is abundant, varied and fascinating.

Birds of America, the collection that was Audubon's masterpiece, features memorable images of Florida's most beloved birds. While the artist was traveling in Florida, he observed more than fifty species of birds that he had never before seen in his life. As a modern birdwatcher would say, Audubon added more than fifty birds to his "life list" during his Florida travels, as well as finding opportunities for a closer study of many species that he had glimpsed before. For this beloved artist whose work has fostered such appreciation for birds and their environments, Florida was a rewarding destination.

Audubon was not the first nature artist in Florida; he was well aware of his predecessors, especially William Bartram, a Pennsylvania Quaker who visited Florida during the eighteenth century. Bartram was a true adventurer; during his journey, he canoed across a lake full of alligators, surviving to tell the tale and sketch the creatures. His descriptions of alligators in Florida were widely read during his time, and they provoked both astonishment and skepticism. Yet many of his observations about these great reptiles have since been confirmed; Bartram was a keen observer.

The book that Bartram wrote about his travels, which was accompanied by his sketches, was a remarkable combination of natural history and poetic flair. It attracted the attention of such varied readers as George Washington, Thomas Jefferson and the English poet Samuel Taylor Coleridge. William Bartram is also noteworthy for his respect for Native American cultures and his friendly dealings with the tribes he encountered. The famous Seminole chieftain Ahaya, or "Cowkeeper," gave Bartram the name the "Flower Hunter." There might have been a touch of humor about the epithet, but it was also a unique tribute to his treks through the forest in search of botanical curiosities.

Florida seemed like an unexplored wilderness to William Bartram; however, another artist had chronicled its natural wonders at an even earlier period. Mark Catesby was a Royal Society man who sailed from England during the early 1700s. For him, Florida, and indeed all of America, was truly a new world.

When Catesby returned to London, he published a book titled *The Natural History of Carolina, Florida, and the Bahama Islands*, featuring colorful images of birds, fish, flowers and trees that were found in the new frontiers he had explored. Catesby knew that artwork would make the book more meaningful, but he was not a trained artist. The eccentric style that resulted is part of his appeal. In one image, Catesby shows a flamingo side by side with a piece of coral. A viewer might wonder, why is the coral on land? And what about the lack of scale? Is that an enormous piece of coral or a very tiny flamingo? Yet taken by themselves, both the flamingo and the coral are portrayed with care and accuracy. Catesby's artwork is unique, and it reflects a sense of excitement and discovery.

Each of these three artists was, in his own way, an explorer of nature in Florida. This book is an invitation to join them on their adventures. It will tell the stories behind beautiful and historic works of art portraying Florida's birds and animals. And it will invite the reader to share in the sense of wonder that inspired these artists on their journeys, for to observe nature with appreciation is indeed to be "increasingly amazed."

In the 1720s, Mark Catesby pioneered the study of natural history in Florida. In the 1770s, William Bartram visited St. Augustine, traveled on the St. John's River and explored the area near Gainesville that is today known as Paynes Prairie Preserve State Park. According to the Bartram Trail Conference, his journey took him to points as far south as Sebastian and as far west as Newberry. In the 1820s, John James Audubon visited St. Augustine and sailed along the St. John's, as well as making voyages to the Keys and the Dry Tortugas.

These are their stories.

1
FROM LONDON TO FLORIDA

Catesby and the Royal Society

The foggy streets of London seem far away from the sun-dappled greenery of Florida. Yet in one of London's great cultural landmarks, the British Museum, a special place is given to the work of an artist who was inspired by Florida's natural beauty.

Mark Catesby was a fellow of the Royal Society; his work is connected with the history of the British Museum, and his colorful images of subtropical flora and fauna opened up new horizons to his eighteenth-century English contemporaries. For them, the art of Mark Catesby was a glimpse into the New World.

Walking through the Enlightenment Gallery in the British Museum is like traveling through the history of civilization at whirlwind speed. The grand classical architecture of the gallery, with its towering marble columns, houses a vast range of artifacts. Ancient Greek and Roman statuary, a small-scale Egyptian sphinx from the time of the pharaohs, an astrolabe from the Middle Ages, a wooden shield made by Australian aborigines, blue-and-white Chinese ceramics, natural objects like giant nautilus shells—all can be found there. Bookshelves with leather-bound, gold-engraved volumes line the walls. Some of the books are opened, displayed in such a way that their illustrations can be viewed. And amid all these treasures, the image of a scarlet ibis—a flamboyantly colored tropical bird—can be seen; the bird seems to peek out from the pages of an open book as if curious about the gallery.

Why are these artifacts all in one room when the vast museum has numerous specialized galleries? It's because these treasures represent the origins of the British Museum. Their origins span the globe, but they all ended up in the collections of eighteenth-century Englishmen like the museum's founder, Sir Hans Sloane. Men like Sir Hans had eclectic interests, high education and vast wealth; prized items from all over the world ended up on their estates. These collections were the foundation of the British Museum, and the Enlightenment Gallery itself was originally designed as a library for King George III. Of course, there were some nefarious stories behind some of these treasures and collections; a portion of Sir Hans's money (the part that came from his wife's family) was made from West Indian plantations worked with slave labor, not to mention the question of who might have quarried the stone for the Pharaoh's sphinx or the marble used by the Greek and Roman sculptors. Taken for all in all (as Shakespeare would say), the collection of the Enlightenment Gallery, while somewhat random, may be about as complete a look at world history as the visitor is ever likely to see assembled in a single room. It chronicles the triumphs and tragedies, the crimes and the aspirations and the scientific and artistic achievements of the human story.

What, though, is the scarlet ibis doing here? It is a beautiful bird that is found in the Caribbean and various South American countries, including Colombia and Ecuador. It is also, sometimes, a visitor to Florida, though the state is outside its usual range; two of its relatives—the white ibis and the glossy ibis—are of course familiar birds of Florida.

But this particular scarlet ibis is peeking out from the pages of Mark Catesby's book, an original copy of *The Natural History of Carolina, Florida, and the Bahama Islands*, displayed in the Enlightenment Gallery, opened to the illustration of the colorful bird. Not only is this a fascinating place to see Catesby's work displayed, but it is also a setting that provides insight into the artist's own background, his life story and his life's work.

THE SQUIRE SETS FORTH

Does *The Natural History of Carolina, Florida, and the Bahama Islands* sound like a lengthy title? This was the eighteenth century, an age of lengthy titles, and it is in fact an abbreviated name. The full title is *The Natural History of Carolina, Florida, and the Bahama Islands: Containing the Figures of Birds, Beasts, Fishes, Serpents, Insects and Plants: Particularly the Forest-Trees, Shrubs, and other Plants, not hitherto Described, or very incorrectly figured by Authors. Together with their Descriptions in English and French.* Those were the days!

Had its author been of a less adventurous turn, he might easily have spent his life as a squire of the English countryside, leading a peaceful but forgotten existence. His family had lands in Essex and Suffolk; the will of his father, who died in 1703, makes it clear that they were prosperous. The document reveals that John Catesby bequeathed to his son Mark a number of houses, gardens and orchards in the country, along with multiple houses in London. The Catesbys were neither famous nor aristocratic, but they were certainly very comfortable.

Another surviving artifact from Catesby's life is a book that he owned, an illustrated edition of Aesop's *Fables*. (He wrote his name in the book.) There were over one hundred illustrations in this edition, portraying all kinds of animals. Of course, Aesop's animals are anthropomorphized, and his fables are really about human nature. But it is intriguing that Catesby, whose own great achievement would be an illustrated book that portrayed animals scientifically, had a book of illustrated animal fables in his own library.

Catesby was fascinated by nature throughout his life. In the preface to *The Natural History of Carolina, Florida, and the Bahama Islands* he writes of having had an "early Inclination" that led him "to search after plants and other productions in nature." (Spelling, and to some extent grammar, have been modernized in quotes from Catesby's *Natural History*.) Eventually, that interest led him to travel. "My curiousity was such, that not being content with contemplating the Products of our own Country, I soon imbibed a passionate desire of viewing Animal as well as Vegetable productions in their native countries; which were strangers to England." So, he had curiosity and a spirit of adventure. But with the wide world before him, where would he go?

Because of a family connection, the initial answer was Virginia. By 1712, Catesby was in colonial Williamsburg with his sister and brother-in-law. The brother-in-law was a physician, Dr. William Cocke, who also dabbled in trade and politics, serving in various positions within the colonial administration of Virginia. The family met William Byrd II, a prominent citizen of the colony, and visited his estate. Byrd's diary contains some references to his visitor, and one note in particular is of considerable interest in giving us a glimpse of Catesby's early observations of North American wildlife.

Byrd relates an occasion where the Cocke-Catesby clan enjoyed a fine meal at his estate. After dinner, he took his guests "into the swamp to see the nest of a hummingbird....We found a nest with one young and one egg in it." The hummingbird is an amazing creature that is distinct to the New World; the more than three hundred species known today are all found in the Americas. For Catesby, as an enthusiast of natural history new to the American shores, this must have been an exciting moment. He would later portray a hummingbird in his *Natural History*, showing it sipping nectar from a flower. Catesby titled the illustration *The Humming-Bird, the Trumpet-Flower*. Note his use of the definite article; to him, this was *the* hummingbird. To viewers today, the bird is clearly recognizable as a ruby-throated hummingbird; the accompanying description Catesby provides corroborates this identification, for he mentions "the whole throat adorned with feathers placed like the scales of a fish, of crimson metallic resplendency." From Catesby's perspective, the very existence of a hummingbird—a tiny, acrobatic creature with wings that beat so quickly they seem a blur, iridescent feathers that glitter in the sunlight and the ability to fly backward and upside down—was amazing (as indeed it is). So, his picture was of *the* hummingbird. How could he have imagined that there are over three hundred different species?

During the time of his visit to Virginia, it seems that Catesby was not yet contemplating the production of his *Natural History*. He later wrote that during this time, he enjoyed following his inclination to admire curious plants and animals, and he even sent some back as specimens to friends in England, but that was as far as his scientific pursuits went. It was only later that his desire to share his discoveries would become more intent—and that his gaze would turn south.

VOYAGES OF DISCOVERY

Catesby is believed to have visited the West Indies in 1714 before returning to Virginia; a few years later, in the autumn of 1719, he returned to England and spent about two and a half years in his homeland before making another voyage to the New World. The time spent back on English soil, while relatively brief, was important to Catesby's career. On his first voyage, he had been an enthusiastic dilettante, visiting family in a colony and observing nature in between glasses of wine at the tables of wealthy citizens. On his second voyage, Catesby was a scientific explorer, traveling for the purposes of natural history research and exploration. What had changed?

Perhaps Catesby himself had changed, for a start. He had matured; the love for nature that he always had might have begun to seem charged with purpose, giving a sense of direction to a life that had otherwise been easygoing—maybe too easygoing. Catesby's writing is deliberately impersonal, so it is difficult to be sure. We do know, however, that his time in England won him some important friends, or at least some important allies. One of the botanists to whom he had sent specimens and correspondence shared some of his letters about Virginia with a colleague, Dr. William Sherard. In turn, Sherard encouraged Catesby to make another trip to the New World.

Dr. Sherard moved in exalted circles, and he was important in the web of patronage that characterized eighteenth-century natural history studies. This was an age when the latest scientific theories were discussed in coffeehouses and butterfly collections were examined over glasses of port. With Sherard's interest came the interest of other gentlemen who had the motive, the means and the opportunity to encourage voyages of discovery. Among them was Sir Hans Sloane. A duke and two earls are also singled out for thanks in Catesby's book. The enthusiastic squire had found his place in a very specialized world.

At this time, he was not yet a fellow of the Royal Society—that would come later—but he was traveling under the society's aegis. The Royal Society was the most exalted body of scientific inquiry in Great Britain; it was founded in the seventeenth century with King Charles II as its patron. Sir Isaac Newton was an early president. The organization still exists today; its most famous modern fellow is probably Sir David Attenborough, who has written about Catesby's work and who, in his enthusiasm and sense of exploration, is someone Catesby might well relate to.

Catesby's new voyage brought him not to Virginia but to Charleston, South Carolina. From that starting point, he spent the next four years in the travels and explorations that would lead to the illustrated book that is his legacy. With the title—*The Natural History of Carolina, Florida, and the Bahama Islands*—Catesby announced to the world that Florida had been part of his field of exploration. The map that he would feature in the book implies this, as well. Titled *A Map of Carolina, Florida, and the Bahama Islands with the Adjacent Parts*, it shows Florida with some degree of accuracy, the panhandle above and the peninsula below; however, the peninsula is overly wide. An early advertisement for the book states that the author had traveled through "various Parts of Florida." The geographical vagueness is typical, and determining Catesby's exact route in Florida is impossible.

There are several reasons for that. For one thing, the boundaries between Florida, Georgia and Carolina were by no means clearly delineated. In his preface, Catesby refers to having spent "almost three years in Carolina and the adjacent parts, which the Spaniards call Florida, particularly that province lately honoured with the name of Georgia." Like the names themselves, the question of where the borders were drawn reflected rivalries between Spain (which held Florida) and Great Britain (which held the Carolinas and Georgia). Resolving such questions was a matter of international politics far beyond the purview of a natural historian.

Furthermore, trying to trace the route of Catesby's travels in just about any territory is problematic. His *Natural History* is written like a dictionary of New World zoology and botany; there are descriptions of plants and animals, but they are very succinct, more like captions for the illustrations than stories in themselves. Even the longest entries are generally confined to scientific facts, with occasional asides about how a plant can be used in agriculture or whether a fish tastes good.

Authorial persona—or lack thereof—is a key distinction between Catesby and the artist-naturalists who came after him. William Bartram and John James Audubon were great storytellers, and they were willing to be characters in their own stories; Audubon even made up a flamboyant persona for himself as the "American Woodsman," dressing in buckskins and acting as if he had stepped out of *The Last of the Mohicans*, despite his French upbringing and education. In contrast, the personality of Mark Catesby remains elusive, as does the route of his journey. Perhaps he placed a high value on scientific detachment and wanted to draw no attention to himself beyond the initials FRS (Fellow of the Royal Society), which he would eventually be able to write following his name. Perhaps he was simply a very private man, guarded and careful about what he shared with the public. No known portrait of him survives. Or perhaps this mysterious character simply wanted his art to stand alone.

Treasure Map

The map that Catesby included as part of his *Natural History* is a work of art in itself. Florida is portrayed in bright yellow, as if Catesby was anticipating its future nickname as the Sunshine State. The name is hyphenated and appears as "Flori-da." This is not because it was actually spelled that way in the time—even in the variable spellings of the eighteenth century, Florida was consistently one word—but because it seems he ran out of room in the unmarked areas of the peninsula's interior. The map is abundant in bright colors. Cuba is also in yellow; the Bahamas, Georgia and the Carolinas are in pink; Louisiana and Virginia are in green. Much of the Caribbean is shown, as is the Gulf of Mexico as far as the Yucatan. For Catesby, this was a treasure map. The treasure was not gold doubloons but the natural wonders to be discovered in areas that he had explored or wished to explore.

What of Florida landmarks? St. Augustine is of course included, along with nearby Matanzas Inlet. Much of the interior of Florida was unexplored wilderness in Catesby's day, so a dearth of settlements or landmarks there is not surprising. Most of the Florida landmarks Catesby gives are water features: bays, inlets and rivers. The Florida Keys appear off the south coast of the peninsula, although they are clustered somewhat haphazardly, and they are unnamed. Gulf Coast landmarks include several bays and rivers, and along the coast of the panhandle, the locations of Spanish fortresses are noted.

Although Florida was part of the Spanish empire, British interest in the region is reflected in Catesby's map; he has placed a dotted line well south of St. Augustine with a label that would have been internationally controversial at the time. The label reads: "The Southern Bounds of Carolina by the last charter." Thus, the map implicitly claims northern Florida, including St. Augustine, as British colonial territory—a claim unlikely to be recognized in Madrid.

Regardless of how far Catesby did or did not travel in Florida, there is good reason for including him in a consideration of historical artists of nature in Florida. The Florida Museum does so; its archive Artist-Naturalists in Florida includes an article about Catesby and his patrons (written by Charlotte M. Porter) as well as a selection of his works. As an artist, Catesby portrayed many species that are found in Florida, regardless of whether he himself observed them on Floridian soil, in other southern colonies or in the Bahamas. His self-chosen title proclaimed his interest in Florida and promoted Florida to his European audiences. Finally, his work proved to be an inspiration to William Bartram, who certainly traveled extensively in Florida, as we shall see.

This title banner is a glimpse of Mark Catesby's life and personality. Written on a field of blue and surrounded by seashells, it declares, "*A Map of* Carolina, Florida, *and the* Bahama Islands with the Adjacent Parts." Above it is a scallop shell, while on either side is a spiral shell; stretching below the title and almost touching (but not quite) are two different types of coral, or perhaps marine plants—the appearance is stylized. All this appears above the waters of the Atlantic Ocean; the right-hand seashell brushes up against the label of Port Royal, Bermuda.

It is a whimsical image that shows imagination and flair and evokes a theme of nautical adventure. Indeed, it looks like a maritime version of a heraldic coat of arms. Mark Catesby never had a coat of arms, but perhaps this should have been it; a fitting emblem it would be for a man who was an artist, an adventurer and an explorer of nature.

2

"THE BEAUTY OF THEIR COLOURS"

Catesby as an Artist of Nature

The art of Mark Catesby began in the New World and was completed in the Old World.

For any artist of natural history, observation is the beginning of everything. The next step is recording those observations through some method that will serve as a memory aid for the artist. All of this, for Catesby, took place during his explorations in the New World. As he traveled and explored, he sketched and made notes.

Today, the romantic image of an artist inspired by nature is that of painting *en plein air*, completing the entire work outside, immersed in a garden or wilderness environment. However, this idea comes from French impressionists like Claude Monet—thus the French name for the technique—and Catesby was working a century and a half before their time. Furthermore, Catesby's finished works were not paintings but rather printed illustrations for a book. Thus, his process began with notes and sketches from the field, continued with the painting of watercolors and then with engraving and coloring and was finally completed with publication. It was, in truth, the work of a lifetime for him.

The Artist Afield

The field sketches were done with pencils or pen and ink. Sometimes Catesby would include touches of watercolor to indicate the correct color of his natural subjects, while in other cases, he would make written notes regarding color descriptions. The expression *field sketches* is apt because these works were done during his expeditions as memory aids; it does not indicate that they were all literally done in the field, since botanical subjects, in particular, were collected as specimens and might be sketched at leisure in a room of an inn.

Of the Catesby sketches that have survived, some of them are found on the reverse side of his completed watercolors. For the watercolors themselves, Catesby generally began with a graphite sketch, followed by pen and ink, followed by multiple layers of color; lastly, he would use a delicate brush with additional pigment for fine details. These beautiful and detailed watercolors, while works of art in themselves, would serve as the basis for the engraving, printing and coloring of the illustrations in his book.

Although Catesby is reticent with autobiographical information and details of his travels, the preface of his *Natural History* does provide insight into his work as an artist of nature. His love of birds and his desire to convey the natural artistry of their plumage is certainly evident. "There is greater variety of the feather'd Kind than of any other Animals," he writes, with the poetic flair of his era. "They excel in the Beauty of their Colours." His interests in birds and botany overlapped, and he tried to show birds near plants that were their food sources or were otherwise part of their natural habitat. Furthermore, Catesby painted birds "while they were alive," thereby enabling him to observe their habits and activities as well as their appearance—he writes of trying to show them with the "gestures" that were distinct to their kinds.

Catesby was addressing the challenges faced by all artists who wish to portray birds. Imagine painting a portrait of a human subject and trying to convince your model to stay still. Now imagine trying to sketch or paint a bird. Some artists abandoned such attempts and worked from specimens, that is, birds that had been hunted for the purpose of studying their preserved remains. Much was lost, of course, in comparison to observing the living creatures. A nineteenth-century German English artist named Joseph Wolf once wrote that an artist who worked only from specimens could never "know the true color of the eyes." Audubon (as we shall see) would strive for what he thought was the best of both worlds by combining the field observation of living birds with the use of specimens as models. Catesby, however, used specimens only in "a very few" instances, preferring to work purely for life when it came to birds.

He did rely on specimens for fish, but he was concerned about the way their colors faded when they were "out of their Element." He would therefore try to get fresh specimens if he was still working while this was happening. He admits, though: "I do not pretend to have had this advantage in all, for some kinds I saw plenty of, and of others I never saw above one or two." Reptiles he found comparatively easy to keep alive in captivity and therefore notes that he "had no difficulty in painting them" from life.

For plants, as well as shells and corals, Catesby certainly worked from specimens, and he also passed such specimens along to his patrons. Rare specimens, along with sketches, were a way that he could repay them for their professional and financial interests in his voyages. At times, however, the requests of such patrons seemed demanding; Catesby would ruefully note, in a letter to Sir Hans Sloane, that he had not realized he would be expected to obtain specimens for so many people when he also needed specimens that he could keep as a basis for his artwork.

Patrons and Royalty

Another problem Catesby had with his patrons was that their generosity only went so far. When he returned from his voyages and sought to publish his work in England, he found that the encouragement this time was verbal rather than financial. Although they had helped to fund his travels, they were not willing to directly finance his publishing venture. Instead, Catesby had to line up subscriptions, as was often the case with such enterprises. Each subscriber paid a fee, which was a kind of down payment for a purchase of the book; this raised money for printing costs and allowed the author to assess the market. Catesby's book was published in multiple parts, allowing the subscription strategy to continue and thereby giving him the resources to complete what would be a monumental work. The parts were designed so that they could eventually be bound together as a completed volume.

The book was very expensive; production costs made that inevitable. It was aimed at a true niche audience—wealthy natural history enthusiasts—but that was the audience Catesby had been cultivating for years. Sir Hans, for example, ordered several copies, including the one now displayed in the Enlightenment Gallery of the British Museum.

The book would even interest royalty. Catesby included a dedication to Queen Caroline and, in 1729, presented the first volume to that lady. His audience with the queen would be noted in various newspapers, doubtless adding to the interest in his work. Queen Caroline (the wife of King George II) was an intelligent woman, and Catesby's dedication speaks of her "great

Goodness in encouraging all sorts of learning." While such addresses are easy to dismiss as mere flattery, Catesby's dedication to the queen is actually a poetic and interesting piece of writing that reflects the sense of exploration that motivated his work. He expresses how the natural wonders that his book shows have "hitherto lain concealed from the view of Your MAJESTY." That is, they were waiting to be discovered. The dedication also shows a spiritual aspect of Catesby's view of natural history (something corroborated by other statements in the text of the book). He writes of "the Glorious Works of the Creator, displayed in the New World." For Catesby, to study nature was to gain insight into the wisdom of God. This was also to prove a powerful motivation for William Bartram, and it is a principle that would animate Audubon's writings as well.

Matters of patronage, royal and otherwise, were important in making Catesby's book a success, but our artist also had to deal with the fact that he had not, in actual fact, been trained as an artist. Catesby's endeavor was therefore a daring one. With his country squire background, he had probably had some tutoring in sketching and watercolors during his youth, which he put to use in his field studies. He had learned much through trial and error while sketching specimens. But when he began lining up subscriptions for his *Natural History*, he was committing himself to turn these sketches into a lavishly illustrated book suitable for the grandest libraries in England.

"ILLUMINATING NATURAL HISTORY"

One might wonder why Catesby chose such a bold approach. Why not just *write* about what he had seen? He answers that question in his preface, declaring that the "Illuminating of Natural History" is "essential to the perfect understanding of it." By "Illuminating," he means illustrating; it is of interest that he chooses a word so associated with the history of illustrated books. (Think of the illuminated manuscripts of the Middle Ages, which often featured colorful images of animals as characters in fables or figures in heraldry.) "A clearer Idea may be conceived from the Figures of Animals and Plants in their proper colours, than from the most exact Description without them." It is a simple yet profound argument for the union of natural history and art.

Aware of the challenge before him, Catesby sought the help of someone more experienced: Joseph Goupy, a London painter and engraver. This "inimitable Painter" taught Catesby the art of engraving through "kind advice and Instructions," so the preface courteously informs us. For his images of birds, Catesby sought to adapt the techniques of engraving to "the humour of the Feathers"—that is, their natural composition and form. Even though doing so was more laborious, he hoped that it also proved "more to the purpose."

In addition to Goupy's mentoring, Catesby benefitted from the association of Georg Ehret, a German artist living in London who was celebrated for his botanical images. Catesby and Ehret collaborated, with Ehret contributing some watercolors and two etchings (all based on Catesby's own studies) to the elaborate production process of *Natural History*. Catesby also became friends with the great English natural history painter George Edwards. Edwards contributed some drawings to *Natural History*; in turn, Catesby shared his newfound knowledge of engraving with Edwards. They remained friends throughout Catesby's life, and their conversations about nature and art must have been fascinating and lively. Edwards was a major artistic chronicler of British and European birds, as Catesby was of the birds of the New World.

The skills that Catesby learned in engraving were essential to him; however, it was the brilliant colors he used that brought his work to life. How did Catesby bring color into his artistic process? To a modern audience, the answer might seem mind-boggling. For every illustration in every copy, Catesby added the colors by hand.

What was the scale of this project? There were about 160 copies of the book. In each book, there were 220 of Catesby's hand-colored works of art. That means that Catesby had more than 35,000 images to color. Of course, each book was expensive—it would have to be! And each subscriber was a person of note. Nevertheless, it was painstaking work on a monumental task. There can be no doubt that this elaborate project of hand-coloring thousands of images was an amazing testament to Catesby's perseverance.

Color was of great interest and importance to him, both as an artist and as a natural historian. Recall why he took such care in observing and painting birds—because of "the beauty of their colours." Also, it was Catesby's method to portray the male birds in his illustrations, while simply describing the females in the text, because "Males of the Feather'd Kind (except a very few) are more elegantly coloured than the females."

With all of his color selections, Catesby tried to make choices that were true to life and that would last. "Of the paints, particularly Green, used in the illumination of Figures, I had principally a regard to those most resembling Nature, that were durable and would retain their luster." He knew that all that glitters is not gold. He rejected pigments that were "very specious and shining, but of an unnatural colour and a fading quality."

Travel and exploration, close observation from life, sketches in the field, watercolor paintings, the study of engraving, a striving for realism, careful color selection, patient hand-coloring—all of that went into each one of Mark Catesby's illustrations for *Natural History*. With what rewards? Let us consider some of Catesby's images of birds familiar in Florida, and we shall see.

3

THE IBIS, THE FLAMINGO AND THE CORAL

Images from Catesby's Work

Having already glimpsed the scarlet ibis peeking out into the galleries of the British Museum, let us consider its Floridian relatives. Catesby portrayed the white ibis in two different images for his *Natural History*. This bird is familiar throughout Florida, in part because it has adapted so well to human presence; it is common to see flocks of white ibises on lawns and golf courses. The most recognizable feature of this bird is its long, curved bill. This is believed to be the reason that the ancient Egyptians associated the ibis of the Nile River (now called the African sacred ibis) with their god of scribes; the bill might have reminded them of the writing implements used by their scribes, which in turn led to ibises being revered and mummified.

Such ancient superstitions were a far cry from Catesby's scientific perspective; he analytically noted the measurements of the white ibis's bill in his text, adding that it is "channeled from the base to the point." He portrays all this quite accurately in the illustration. Along with its accuracy, however, the image is a fine example of Catesby's use of color and the importance of color in his work—from both an artistic and scientific standpoint.

Ibises Young and Old

With the white ibis, Catesby dramatically showed the contrast between the bright orange color of the distinctive bill and the bright white of its plumage.

It is a fine example of Catesby's interest in color. Even the use of white is striking; it is not simply a blank area of negative space on the paper, nor yet a creamy off-white, but a brilliant and fresh white, tinged with gray to show the outline of the wings and suggest shading.

In fact, Catesby's use of color in this illustration might have a significance that the artist himself was unaware of. It is likely that he was portraying the white ibis during its breeding season. On the portion of the face near the bill, a white ibis has a featherless area; for most of the year, this area is redder and deeper in color than the orange bill. However, during breeding season, both the bill and the featherless area on the face are a vivid orange red. Catesby portrays this brilliancy of color, and he does not show a distinction in color between the bill and the face. This suggests that his white ibis was in its breeding season. The bright white of the plumage would corroborate this, since the change is preceded by molting, and an ibis in this condition would therefore have fresh new feathers.

Birds are often called by different names over time; in Catesby's day, the ibis was known as the curlew. He calls the white ibis the white curlew and the scarlet ibis the red curlew. In some cases, the changes in names over the years

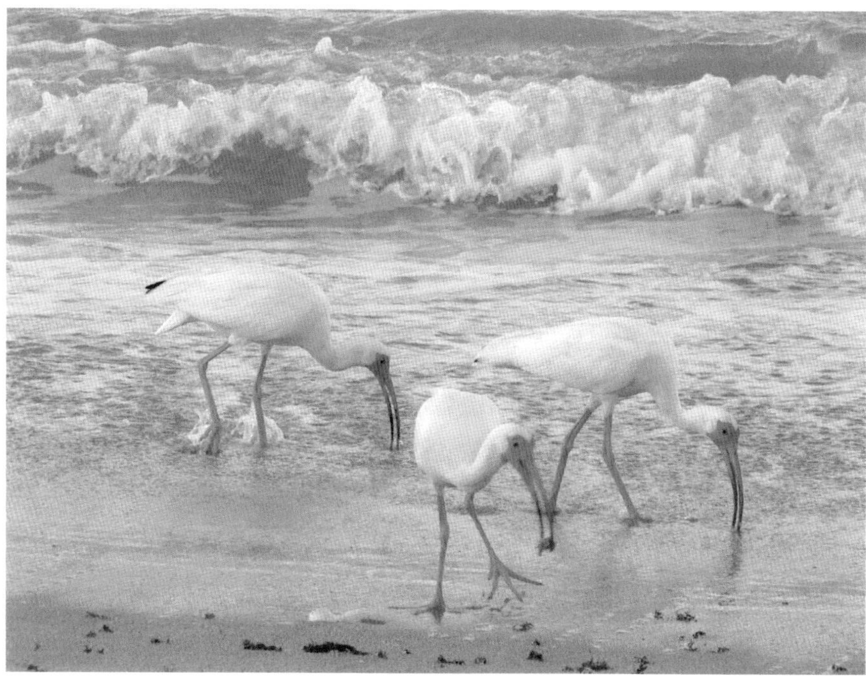

White ibises on a Florida beach. *Author's collection.*

can make it a challenge to identify what species a historical nature writer or nature artist is referring to, but the ibis is quite distinctive by any name.

It was unusual for Catesby, with his encyclopedic approach, to provide two different images of the same species. With the white ibis, however, he made a mistake that many travelers in Florida have made. Juvenile white ibises are brown in color, their plumage flecked with white; the white becomes more and more pronounced as they mature, until they have grown up and attained their white coloring. Catesby understandably thought that young ibises were a separate species, which he called the brown curlew and portrayed with its own illustration and entry in his *Natural History*. He was aware that there was a close resemblance between ibises with these different color patterns, and at first, he thought that the white birds were male and the brown birds were female, or vice versa. However, when he found that there were male birds in each color pattern, he abandoned this theory and concluded that they were different species—not realizing that the difference was in fact age.

A Bird and a Leaf—Catesby's Lack of Scale

In each case, Catesby's ibis illustration also includes a plant. The juvenile white ibis is paired with a plant that Catesby identifies by its scientific name, today called the arrow arum. The adult white ibis is paired with a plant that Catesby again identifies only by scientific name, and which now has the common name of golden club.

In each instance, the plant is portrayed realistically, yet it is out of sync with the scale of the bird—or else the bird is out of sync with the scale of the plant. Furthermore, in each case the plant is rather artificially posed. A closer look at the image of the adult white ibis, this time focusing on the botanical side of the work of art, will serve to illustrate this curious aspect of Catesby's style.

The golden club with which the adult white ibis is paired is a plant that is native to Florida. It is an aquatic plant with a club-shaped stalk that bears small yellow flowers. Catesby realistically portrays the stalk, with the flowers beginning to bud, and he shows a leaf behind it. The separation of stalk and leaf is yet another point of botanical accuracy. With his keen eye for color, Catesby shows the variations in green, with a darker hue on the leaf. Recall his comment about selecting greens that would most closely resemble those found in nature.

With all of this verisimilitude, however, there is one striking contradiction. Individually, the bird and the plant are each portrayed with careful realism, yet Catesby puts them together without any sense of scale. The leaves of the golden club range from six to twelve inches in length. Catesby poses the leaf behind the white ibis, with its stem on the ground and its tip in the air. A white ibis stands about two feet in height and has a wingspan of over three feet. So, the bird should be bigger than the leaf. However, the leaf towers over the ibis; it looks as if the white bird could use the leaf as a green cloak.

Then there is the artificiality of placement. Although an ibis might readily encounter the golden club plant while feeding in a marshy environment, the plant in the Catesby image is arranged like a specimen in a museum. To viewers today, this can seem like a paradox; the imagery is from nature, but the composition of the illustration is quite artificial. However, it makes sense when we consider Catesby's scientific perspective. He is interested in the botanical and zoological accuracy of each individual species; he chooses to put the bird and the plant together as if to suggest a habitat, but he is not trying to create the illusion of a three-dimensional, real-life environment. This is not a work of art to step into; it is a work of art to study.

Catesby's comments about his methods of work also help us understand the composition. He studied birds by observing the living creatures, but he studied plants by collecting specimens. It would have been easy for him to arrange the leaf on his desk in such a way that the maximum detail would be visible; then he could sketch it, which would lead to the watercolor and then to the engraving and then to the final illustration. However, he was not going to pose a live bird on his desk next to the leaf (although it is entertaining to imagine him trying this). The two subjects, bird and plant, were studied separately and the images were designed separately, even though he placed them together in the finished illustration.

Yet another factor is the great obstacle to his *Natural History*, which we have already seen Catesby facing: his lack of training as an artist. He is quite honest about the effects of this, using the preface to tell the reader, "As I was not bred a Painter I hope some faults in Perspective, and other niceties, may be the more readily excused." By telling us that he was not "bred a Painter," Catesby is admitting that he was not formally trained as an artist before beginning this massive project. Then there are the reasons of scientific study: "Plants, and other Things done in a flat, tho' exact manner, may serve the Purpose of Natural History, better in some measure, than in a more Bold and Painter-like Way." Thus, Catesby acknowledges that his artwork lacks a realistic three-dimensional perspective, and he attributes this both to his lack of training and to his scientific purposes.

The lack of scale, or the quirky use of scale, is a characteristic of Catesby's work, and it is something that often surprises the modern viewer. Although it can seem jarring at first, on consideration, it might actually add to his artwork's appeal. Catesby seems to have been an eccentric man—the eighteenth century was a great age for eccentrics—and that comes through in his artwork. The combination of scientific realism and flamboyant disregard for scale gives us images that bring a whimsical air to natural history.

The Influence of an Adventuress

Whatever the differences in scale, the idea of putting individually accurate images of animals and plants together in a single image is not as self-evident as it may sound. Botanical art and zoological art were overlapping fields, but they were not identical ones. Among Catesby's predecessors in natural history art, some who were focused on animals and birds used generic plants in the background; for example, a realistic bird of a particular species might be poised on the bare branch of an unidentifiable tree. One prominent French artist of natural history, who was contemporary with Catesby, even showed some of his animals posing on classical columns; one of his illustrations makes it look as if an anteater was being honored by the ancient Roman senate.

A nature artist whose work is believed to have influenced Catesby was Maria Sibylla Merian. She was not only a brilliant artist and observer of nature, but she also had a truly adventurous spirit. In 1699, Merian had voyaged from Amsterdam to Surinam, then a Dutch colony. Along with having learned the arts of printing and engraving from her family, she was a self-taught entomologist. And she was fascinated by butterfly metamorphosis. Metamorphosis is a mysterious phenomenon today; how much more so would it have been a mystery in the early eighteenth century?

While she was in Surinam, Merian explored the beautiful rain forest environments of South America, observing such wonders as the blue morpho butterfly with its iridescent azure wings, fluttering through the warm and humid air. What for many residents of the tropics is a perennial irritation—the problem of how to keep insects out of your house—was a source of delight for her. In the meadows and forests of Europe, she had searched carefully for insects to study; in the tropics, they came to her! Of course, she spent ample time in the forests as well, enjoying the abundant and varied creatures to be found in these rich habitats.

Merian's sojourn was cut short by malaria, but when she returned to Europe, she produced a remarkable book called *Metamorphosis Insectorum Surinamensium*, which she dedicated to "all investigators of Nature." The beautiful color palettes not only showed a rich variety of butterflies but also provided glimpses of their life cycle and insight into metamorphosis. For each species, Merian tried to show every stage—egg, caterpillar, chrysalis and adult. She also endeavored to show the host plant for each species in the same image, and her nearly flawless accuracy in this is testament to her skill and devotion as an observer of nature.

We know that Catesby was familiar with Merian's work from direct references that he makes; for example, in his description of the opossum, he mentions that Merian wrote of having seen the creature in Surinam. Merian was primarily focused on entomology, and she was especially interested in the study of metamorphosis, so her sphere of study was much more specific than Catesby's. However, her style of including plants and animals in the same composition, and portraying both in a naturalistic way, is believed to have been an influence on him. Both Merian and Catesby include clearly identifiable plants in the same scenes as beautiful creatures from the animal kingdom. These artists were thus giving their animals a habitat, so to speak, within the work of art—something that Audubon would later do on a more elaborate scale.

The distinctions between Merian and Catesby must be noted as well. Merian's combinations of plants and butterflies are highly rational, whereas Catesby's juxtapositions can seem surprising. Merian was pairing butterflies with their host plants, but Catesby's pairing choices do not necessarily have such clear connections—sometimes they have no connection at all. And then there is that distinctive characteristic of Catesby's work: his lack of scale. The whimsical air that all this can give an image is nowhere more evident than in his portrayal of the flamingo.

A SURPRISING PAIR

When you look at Catesby's flamingo for the first time, you are quite likely to think that it is standing in front of a leafless tree. The flamingo itself is beautiful and unmistakable, with its height, its long neck and its vibrant color. It is a wonderful image—even the individual feathers are highly detailed. But why, you might wonder, does Catesby have it standing in front of a withered tree? And why is the tree leafless? Is it dead? Has it lost its leaves for the winter? Surely that would not happen in any place where a flamingo would be found! Look closer, and you see that there is no hint that these branches ever bore leaves. What kind of a tree is this?

Well, it is not really a tree at all. In the accompanying description, Catesby helpfully informs us that it is a piece of coral. This makes more sense, and at the same time, it's even more confusing. It is a much more realistic portrayal of coral than it would be of a tree. But what is a piece of coral doing on land? It even appears to be growing out of the ground. And then there is the flamingo standing right in front of it. Catesby's habit of ignoring scale seems not only whimsical but almost surreal.

How fascinating it would be to know more about what Catesby thought of his own work! The scientific tone of the text reveals little in this regard. The coral is identified by its Latin name; it is a variety now known as Gorgonian coral. The flamingo is of the West Indian species, also called the greater flamingo. Catesby might have seen it in the Bahamas. (It is now the national bird of the Bahamas.) The next image in *Natural History* shows a close-up of the flamingo's head, with the bill portrayed in great detail, appearing to float in the air in front of another piece of coral. Again, there is a surreal quality to the illustration.

Why the enigmatic pairing of flamingo and coral? What was the artist himself thinking? Was this a playful touch, a suggestion of wry humor? It is mysterious—and it is Mark Catesby at his most memorable.

4

MIGRATORY CREATURES

Catesby as a Natural Historian

Along with being a colorful and eccentric artist, Catesby was a natural historian. As we have seen, studying nature was the purpose of his travels, and indeed he learned his skills as an artist in order to share his findings with the public. In this chapter, we will consider some of Catesby's most important contributions to natural history.

In the scientific world of his day, Catesby was an explorer. Much of the excitement about his book came from the fact that it was describing animals and plants that were new to its European audience. So, it is inevitable that he would play a role in the naming of species. And as a man of the eighteenth century, he was living during the age when such nomenclature was coming into its own.

Picture a birdwatcher of today standing on a Florida beach with binoculars in hand, watching the aerodynamic flight of a seabird diving toward the water in the distance. The birdwatcher takes careful note of the details to decide whether it is a Caspian tern, a Sandwich tern or yet another species. It might be easy to tell that it is a tern, but subtle differences are important to making a species identification. This illustrates an important point about the naming of species.

As the word implies, *species* is a specific definition, a deliberately narrow classification. This helps ornithologists study birds in detail and categorize information. It is also great for birdwatchers—it encourages careful observation, and it makes everyone's "life list" much longer than it would otherwise be.

This also tells you that species distinctions have not been around forever. In ancient times, people took note of different kinds of birds, but they were not usually classifying them according to such subtle distinctions. It was during Catesby's time that species classification as we know it was being developed. And since Catesby's book was the primary source of scientific information regarding many New World creatures, it became a major reference work for this monumental task.

Let us continue to use the tern as an example. During the Middle Ages, an Old English poem called "The Seafarer" referred to the tern using the name *stearn*. That name, with its Danish and Old Norse origins, led to the English name *tern*. In the poem, a wandering sailor describes the cry of the tern on an icy northern coast. Of course, he does not specify whether it is a Caspian tern, a Sandwich tern and so forth. Today, on the other hand, approximately forty species of terns are recognized worldwide. They are all terns, and they are all part of the scientific subfamily *Sterninae*. (Yes, there are echoes of the Old English name there.) What happened in between the mediaeval designation of *stearn* and the modern classification of some forty species? The eighteenth century happened—and in particular, the work of Linnaeus happened.

"Kings Play Chess on Fridays, Generally Speaking"

Carl Linnaeus was a Swedish botanist and natural historian who wrote monumental books seeking to define and classify species of plants and animals around the world. These encyclopedic works were called the *Systema Naturae*, and they were used as the basis for classification. In the tenth edition, for example, Linnaeus gave names and definitions for over 4,300 species. The system of scientific names for species as we know it today is a legacy of Linnaeus's work. Scientists had already been using classical languages to name animals and plants; this allowed for ease of communication between experts from different European countries, since during the antiquity-loving eighteenth century, educated men had extensive knowledge of Latin. Catesby himself coined Latin names for species that he described. Linnaeus refined this technique into a precise and orderly system, which he believed reflected the order of nature. It is because of Linnaeus that generations of students have learned the mnemonic device "kings play chess on Fridays, generally speaking" to remember the system of classification, from general to specific: kingdom, phylum, class, order, family, genus and species. What Melvil Dewey is to libraries, Linnaeus is to botany and zoology.

You might guess that a man with so orderly a mind and such a bent for organization and categories would be an armchair scholar, rather than an adventurer. And you would be correct. Linnaeus was not completely sedentary—as a young man he led a scientific expedition to Lapland, and he later visited Paris and other European centers of learning—but the hazards and discomforts of long sea voyages were definitely not for him. Perhaps memories of the poverty he had endured as a student, when he had used crumpled paper to fill holes in his shoes, made him reluctant to leave the comfort of home and hearth. For much of his career, he was based at the University of Uppsala in his native Sweden. Instead of traveling himself, he encouraged his students to go abroad on expeditions, arranging free passage for them on Dutch East India Company ships and cheering them on with the promise that he would name species after them in upcoming editions of his encyclopedia.

Thus, Linnaeus never traveled to the Americas, and he found Catesby's book a tremendous resource when it came to categorizing North American flora and fauna. For the animal kingdom alone, Linnaeus referenced Catesby's entries 139 times in *Systema Naturae*, and for fifty-two animal species entries, Catesby was his only source of information. Linnaeus seemed to find Catesby's studies of birds especially valuable, using his work for eighty-one bird species and using him as the sole source for thirty-three of those species. Catesby's botanical work was also of great use to Linnaeus, introducing the comparatively sedentary Swede to many species of North American and Caribbean plants. One of these plants is the lily thorn, and fittingly, Linnaeus named not only the species but also the whole genus for Catesby; the *Catesbaea* genus includes a variety of species found in Florida and the Bahamas. Today, Catesby is also commemorated with other scientific names of species, such as *Lithobates catesbeianus*, the American bullfrog.

Through Linnaeus's work, Catesby influenced the whole science of natural history. To this day, the system of scientific names for animals and plants rests on Linnaeus's work; his influence on zoology, botany and all biology was profound. And Catesby, with his studies of American zoology and botany, had been a great influence on Linnaeus.

The explorations and discoveries of Mark Catesby were as fascinating to the scholars of continental Europe as they had been to the great minds and great patrons of England. Indeed, *Natural History of Carolina, Florida, and the Bahama Islands* opened up North American nature studies to the universities, libraries and cultural capitals of the Old World.

Mysteries of Migration

One of Catesby's most important, and most fascinating, contributions to natural history came in a paper that he read and presented to the Royal Society in London. Titled "Of Birds of Passage," it was published in the society's journal, *Philosophical Transactions*, in 1747. *Natural History of Carolina, Florida, and the Bahama Islands* had been produced with the society's blessing, but by now, Catesby was a fellow of the Royal Society, and the valued initials FRS appeared in his byline. The paper itself certainly lived up to the society's distinguished standards, proving to be insightful and far-sighted.

"Of Birds of Passage" was about migration. Consider how mysterious migration still is today—how many unanswered questions there are about the instincts that guide birds and the navigational feats that they achieve on their amazing journeys. Now consider how mysterious migration would have been to an eighteenth-century audience. Of course, people knew that some birds migrated for vast distances; that much has been known since ancient times. The Bible book of Jeremiah refers to the migration of storks, and in ancient Greece, Aristotle wrote about the migration of certain birds. It is one thing, however, to know that some birds can migrate and quite another to know just where the bird you see near your cottage in summer has gone for the winter. How common was migration? Were the birds that seemed to be missing from England during the winter actually traveling great distances? Or were they hiding closer to home?

The last suggestion had the support of many. It seemed logical that, instead of flying over seas, oceans and mountains, birds simply hibernated for the winter, like some mammals do. The suggestion was found in Aristotle's writings, for although he realized that some birds migrated, he also believed that many birds burrowed into holes and spent the cold season in torpor. In Catesby's time, many people in England believed that such hibernations took place underwater. Beneath the frozen surface of a wintry lake, there might be sleeping birds waiting for the warmth and light of spring.

In his paper for the Royal Society, Catesby dismissed such ideas the way Sherlock Holmes might dismiss an absurd theory from Inspector Lestrade. "The Reports of their lying torpid in Caverns and hollow Trees, and of their resting in the same State at the Bottom of deep Waters, are so ill attended, and absurd in themselves, that the bare Mention of them is more than they deserve," he declares in the second paragraph. Tact was evidently not his strong point.

Catesby's paper is a clear defense of bird migration as a widespread phenomenon. He also provided a brilliant observation regarding what really prompts these journeys: "The Want of Food seems to be the chief if not the only Reason of their Migration." Many birds can endure the cold, he explained; the lack of food sources during the winter, and the greater availability of food in warmer climates, was a more important motivation. It is a viewpoint shared by many ornithologists of today. Indeed, "Of Birds of Passage" has been hailed by modern ornithologists and birdwatchers as far ahead of its time. During the intervening centuries, abundant evidence has been found to support Catesby's deductive reasoning on migration.

It is of special interest, then, that the spark of inspiration for this paper had come decades earlier, during Catesby's voyages in the New World, in warm waters not far from the Florida coast. "Lying on the Deck of a Sloop on the North Side of *Cuba*," Catesby heard the calls of birds flying overhead. He identified them by their calls: they were "Rice-Birds," known today as bobolinks. Catesby realized that they were traveling between the southern colonies of North America and the continent of South America; he also knew, from accounts and observations in the colonies, that they would return. The birds were migrating, and Catesby must have listened in wonder as their calls echoed through the night air, harmonizing, perhaps, with the lapping of waves against the hull of his ship and the breath of wind in the sails.

He certainly appreciated the wonder and the mystery of migration. "Tho' the secret Ways by which Instinct guides Birds…are little known to us, yet the Causes of some of their Actions are apparent." This epigrammatic statement near the conclusion of his paper is a fitting close to our consideration of Catesby's work. Mark Catesby was filled with a sense of wonder and a love of exploration. He knew that nature was full of mysteries that he would never be able to solve, yet that only enriched his joy as he discovered what he could.

Some months after he presented his paper, Catesby did something that he had apparently never done before: he married. He was sixty-four years old. There is surely a story behind his marriage to Elizabeth Rowland during what would prove to be the evening of his life, but that story is unknown. He was a guarded and private man to the end. Following a decline in his health and injuries from a fall, he died in December 1749 and was buried in a London churchyard.

Catesby's legacy was *The Natural History of Carolina, Florida, and the Bahama Islands*. It is an amazing and colorful book, the magnum opus of a man who was both artist and natural historian and who had the joy of exploring a New World.

5

"NATURE'S NOBLEMEN"

The Bartrams and British Florida

On a spring morning in 1797, a group of visitors to a botanical garden in Philadelphia noticed a gardener working on a bed of tulips. The gardener was wearing a homespun shirt, breeches and a battered, floppy hat. Despite his unprepossessing appearance, they recognized him as a renowned natural historian and adventurer. This humble gardener was none other than William Bartram, who had once steered his canoe through a lake full of alligators in the Florida wilderness.

They immediately approached him, and as one of the visitors later wrote, "he ceased his work, and entered into conversation with the ease and politeness of nature's noblemen. His countenance was expressive of benignity and happiness. This was the botanist, traveler, and philosopher we had come to see."

The scene is a classic depiction of William Bartram's persona. But to understand why the visitors were so excited to meet this modest figure, we must turn our attention to Bartram's younger days and his explorations of Florida.

Family Gardens

William Bartram was born in 1739, and he grew up in the stimulating environment of the botanical gardens that his father, John, had founded. John was a Pennsylvania Quaker with a largely self-taught expertise in

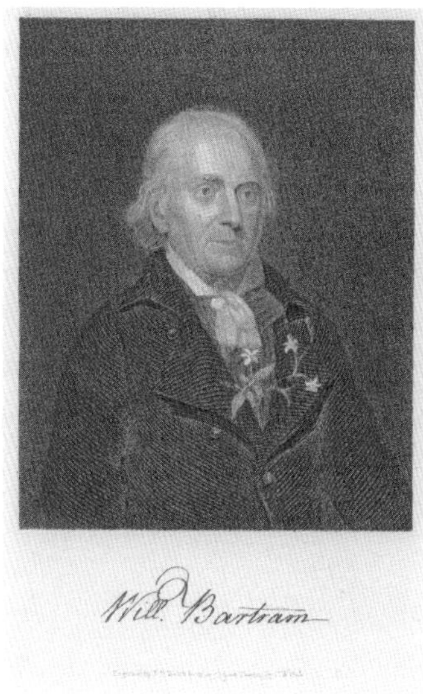

This portrait of William Bartram was based on a painting by Charles Wilson Peale. *Public domain.*

botany. His gardens were an achievement in themselves, as he gathered a collection of North American plants that became the most extensive in the world at that time. He began shipping seeds across the Atlantic to the botanists and gardening enthusiasts of England.

For Philadelphians interested in natural history, the Bartram gardens were a fascinating place to visit, so it was inevitable that Benjamin Franklin would show up. With his scientific curiosity and his witty personality, Franklin was soon a valued friend of the Bartram family. In fact, John became an important early member of Franklin's American Philosophical Society.

The Bartram gardens still exist today. They have been designated a National Historic Landmark. Along with the old stone house, there are fifty acres of parks and gardens, including the current Bartram nursery with its "living collections" that relate to the history of American horticulture.

William's childhood was clearly enriched by such surroundings, and by the time he was fourteen years old, he had begun sketching birds and plants. He became a student at the College, Academy and Charity-School of Philadelphia and eventually a merchant's apprentice; in whatever spare time he could find during those years, he continued his natural history sketches. An image of a magnolia warbler, with a colorful breast of ochre yellow, has survived from those years.

In 1761, William moved to Carolina, where his uncle and namesake, Colonel William Bartram, lived. There, the younger William Bartram set up a trading post, but the business was not prosperous. During the course of his life, he would prove that he had many talents, but business acumen was not among them.

Meanwhile, his father became the recipient of a signal honor. In 1765, John Bartram was appointed royal botanist to the colonies by King George III. This provided motivation for the first Bartram expedition to Florida, which began later that year. Along the way, John stopped at Carolina, where his son William joined him. William must have been excited at the prospect for exploration that the trip held out to him, and his skills in observation and sketching would serve him in good stead. So it was that the Bartrams set forth for the British colony of East Florida at the invitation of the governor.

East Florida, a *British* colony? The story of William Bartram takes us into a period of Florida's history that is little known today. For about twenty years of the nineteenth century, Florida was part of the British Empire. That was the situation not only during the first Bartram expedition to Florida but also during William Bartram's later (and more important) solo trip. Thus, some background about the British period of Florida is clearly in order.

Scottish Hospitality in Florida

The end of a war, a treaty negotiation in Paris, an international deal struck at the table—that was how the British colonial period in Florida began, and it would end in precisely the same way.

The beginning was in 1763; the war that had just ended was known variously as the Seven Years' War, Queen Anne's War and, in North America, the French and Indian War. It was a conflict of colonial powers, and the treaty that was signed would have long-ranging consequences for the colonies themselves. In the north, borders were redrawn as France gave up Canada to the British Empire.

During the war, the British had successfully laid siege to the rich port of Havana, which had been under Spanish dominion. Now, with the war over, the Spanish wanted Havana back, and they were willing to trade the vastly larger—but mostly undeveloped—territory of Florida in exchange for it. During the negotiations for the Treaty of Paris of 1763, the deal was struck, and Florida was transferred from Spanish to British rule.

The British opted to divide their new territory into two separate colonies: West Florida, with Pensacola as a capital, and East Florida, with the old Spanish city of St. Augustine as its capital. Castillo de San Marcos, the coquina fortress in St. Augustine, became known as Fort St. Marks and was manned by a small British garrison. St. Augustine became the initial Florida destination for the Bartram expedition, as it was a natural starting point for further exploration.

Governor James Grant, who at the time was governor of British East Florida, proved himself a welcoming host to the Bartrams. Since John Bartram was a royal botanist, it was only fitting that he be treated hospitably

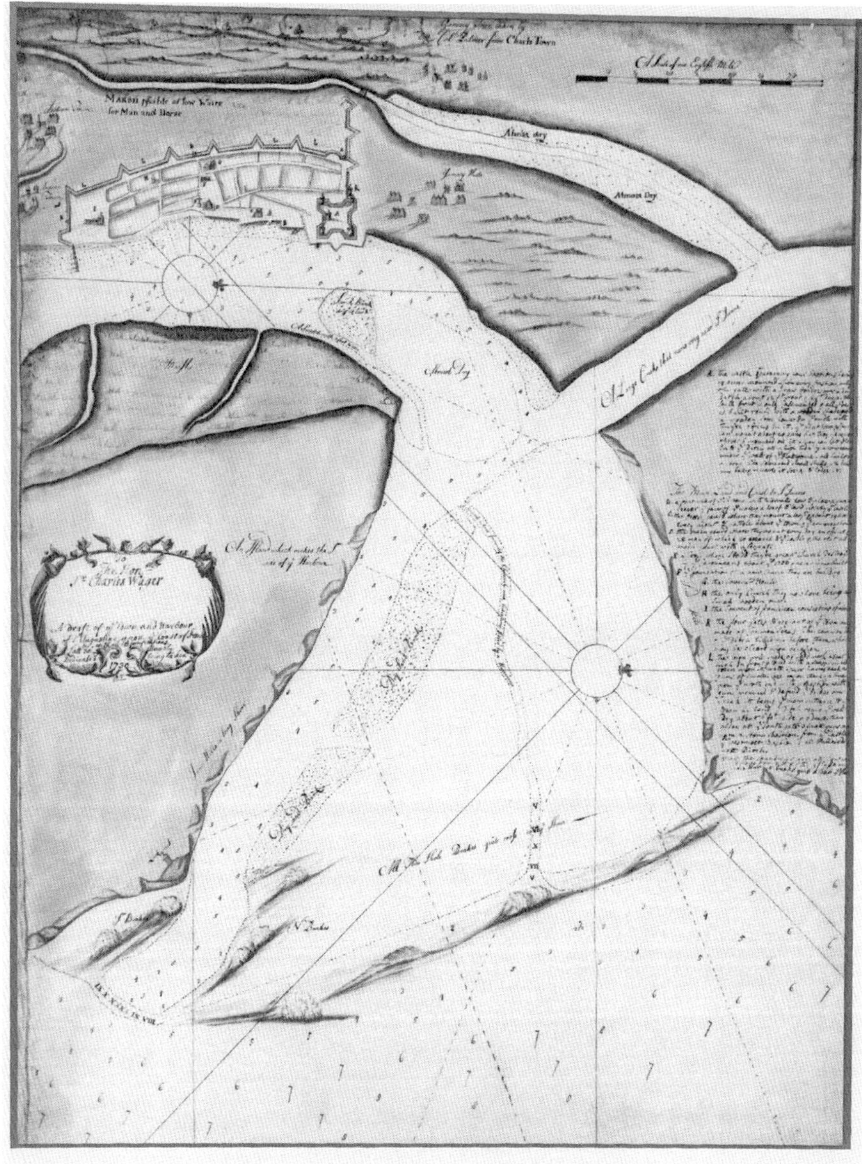

1732 British Spy Map

Drawn by Colonel John Palmer

Colonel John Palmer came from Charles Town in 1732 to spy on the Spanish. Map shows the forts and channels in the St. Augustine harbor.

This map from British Intelligence dates to 1732 and was drawn by a Captain John Palmer; it reflects the colonial rivalries between the British and the Spanish. *NPS photo, public domain.*

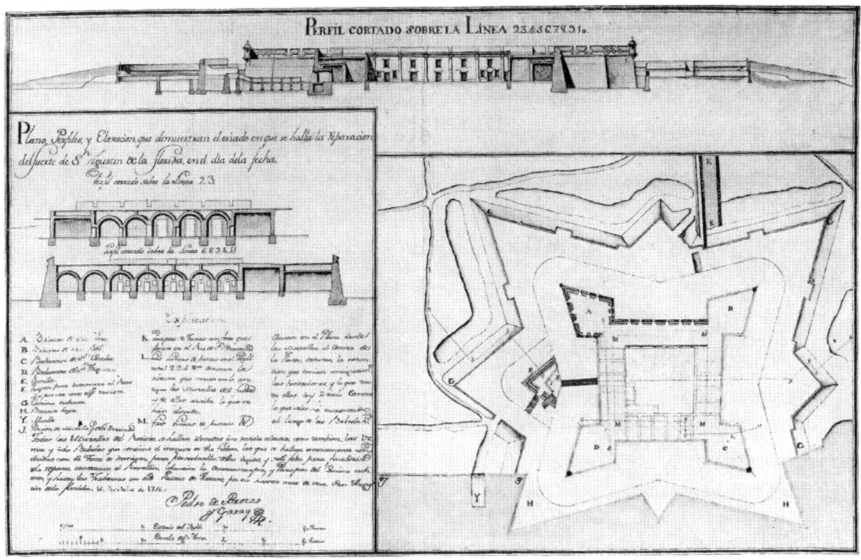

A 1756 plan of the fortress at St. Augustine. *NPS photo, public domain.*

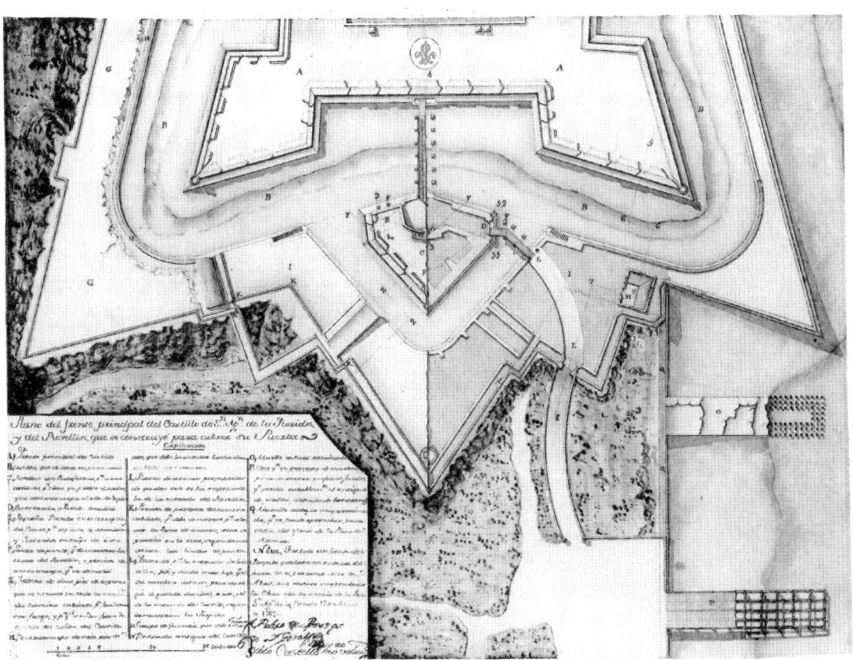

This 1763 image of the fortress shows plans for unfinished defensive modifications. The year 1763 marked the end of the French and Indian War and the beginning of British Florida. *NPS photo, public domain.*

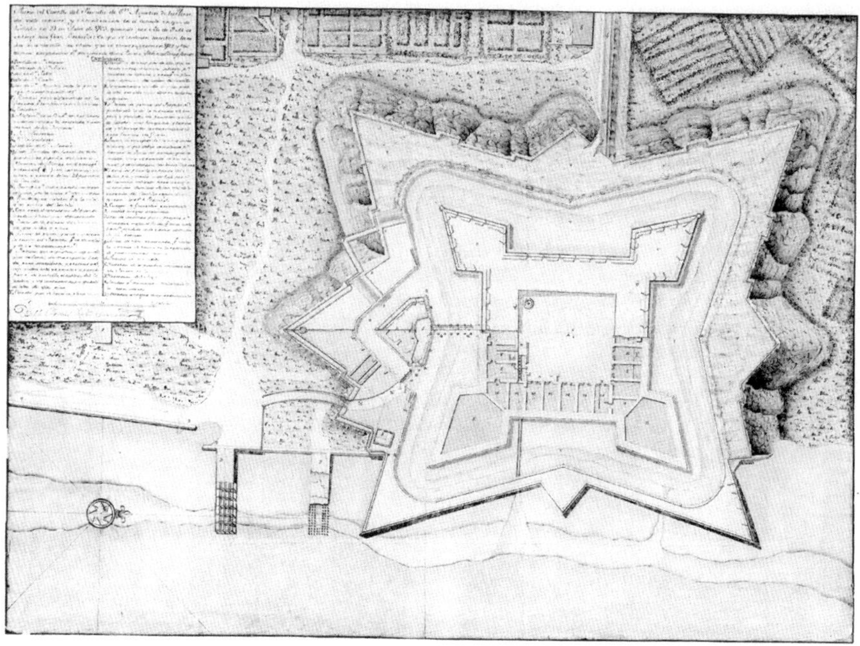

This map showing the fortress and part of the city of St. Augustine dates from 1763. *NPS photo, public domain.*

in what was now a British colony; and Governor Grant was in any case a man renowned for his lavish hospitality.

Grant was born in a castle in the Scottish Highlands—Ballindaloch Castle, which still stands today. Built in the Scottish baronial style, it has ivy-covered walls of gray stone and an oak-paneled dining room with the family crest above the fireplace. The estate on which it stands is known for Angus cattle, good fishing and a single-malt whisky distillery. Fittingly, in view of Grant's support of the Bartrams, it is also a haven for wildlife, with forests that are home to red deer, Scottish wildcats and a colorful bird called the capercaillie—a grouse iconic to Scotland. The castle has been the seat of the lairds of Clan Grant (today Clan Macpherson-Grant) since the 1500s.

James Grant chose to pursue a military career, rising to the rank of major general by the time of the French and Indian War. When he first arrived in British East Florida to take on his responsibilities as governor, the territory must have seemed a world away from his Highland castle home. Regarding his first impressions, Grant said, "The colony was in a state of nature when I found it." Of course, it was precisely that "state of nature" that attracted the Bartrams.

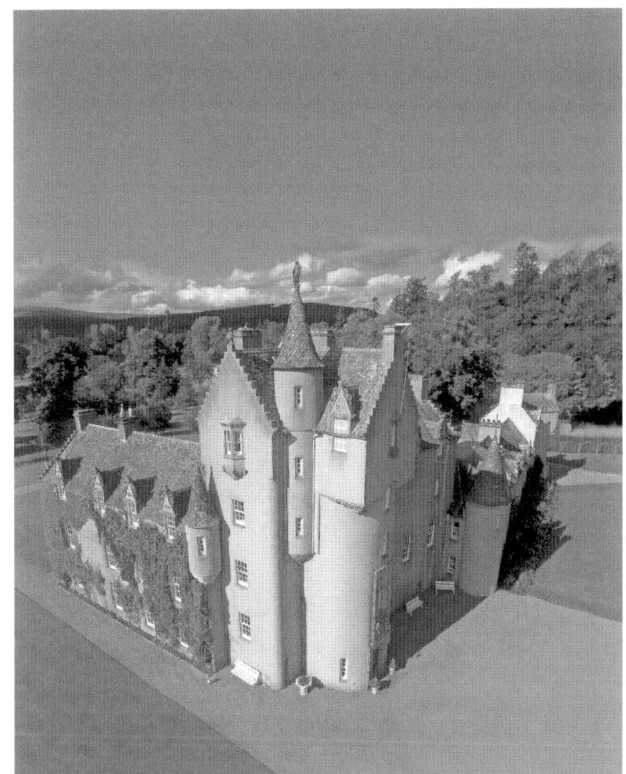

Right: Ballindaloch Castle in Scotland was the ancestral home of Governor James Grant, who provided valuable help and hospitality to the Bartrams. *Courtesy of the Laird Guy Macpherson-Grant.*

Below: Ballindaloch Castle with the daffodil gardens in bloom. *Courtesy of the Laird Guy Macpherson-Grant.*

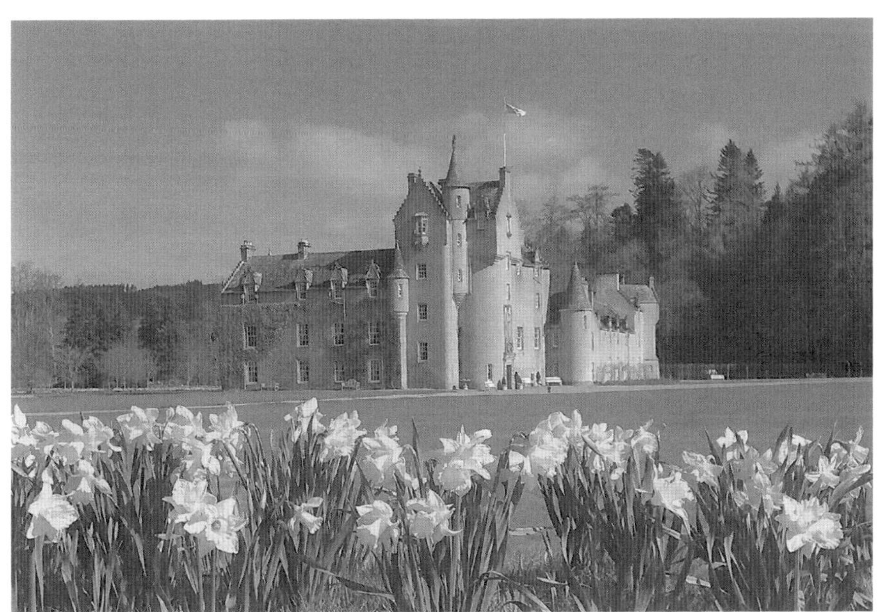

In St. Augustine, Grant lived in what had been the old home of the Spanish governors, a stately residence with a turret, a loggia and a rooftop balcony, and he made sure that it was a place of renowned banquets during his years in the colony. This was both policy and pleasure; the governor thought it would maintain the colony's morale and provide a recompense for living in a place so far removed from the wealthier and more populous centers of British imperial life. Since Grant himself was both a gourmet and gourmand, it is safe to assume that holding banquets was not a particularly onerous task for him; nevertheless, he insisted wryly that it was all part of his duty.

Governor Grant's menu and the wine list can be re-created from surviving inventories. Menu items included lamb, pork, beef, venison, turkey, duck, fish and oysters. Beverage consumption at the governor's banquets during just the first year of Grant's term included 1,200 bottles of claret (a British term for dry red wine from France), 519 bottles of port, 86 gallons of Jamaica rum and 150 gallons of sundry rum. Colony residents who had been on the governor's guest list must have been deeply saddened to see him sail back to Britain at the end of his term.

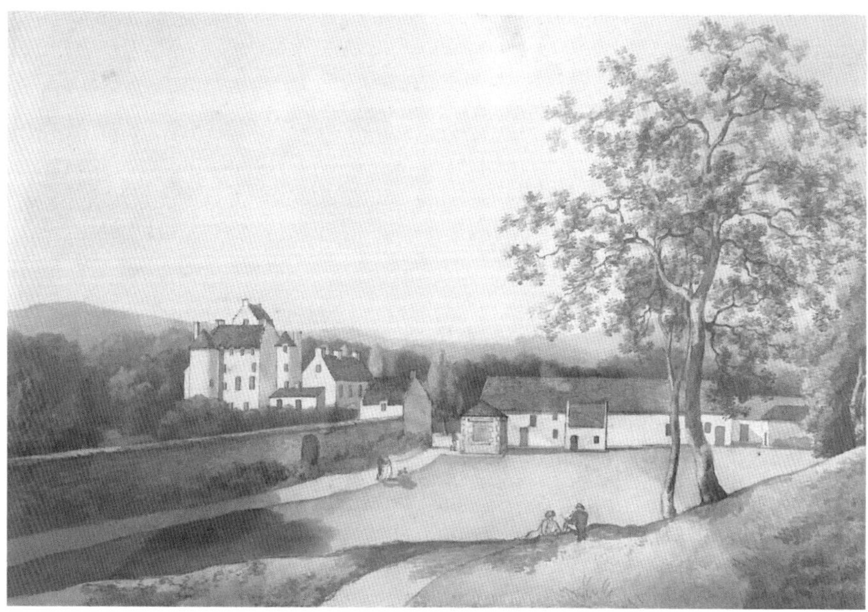

This eighteenth-century watercolor shows how Ballindaloch Castle would have looked in Governor Grant's time. Subsequent to his term in British East Florida, James Grant became the Laird of Ballindaloch. *Courtesy of the Laird Guy Macpherson-Grant.*

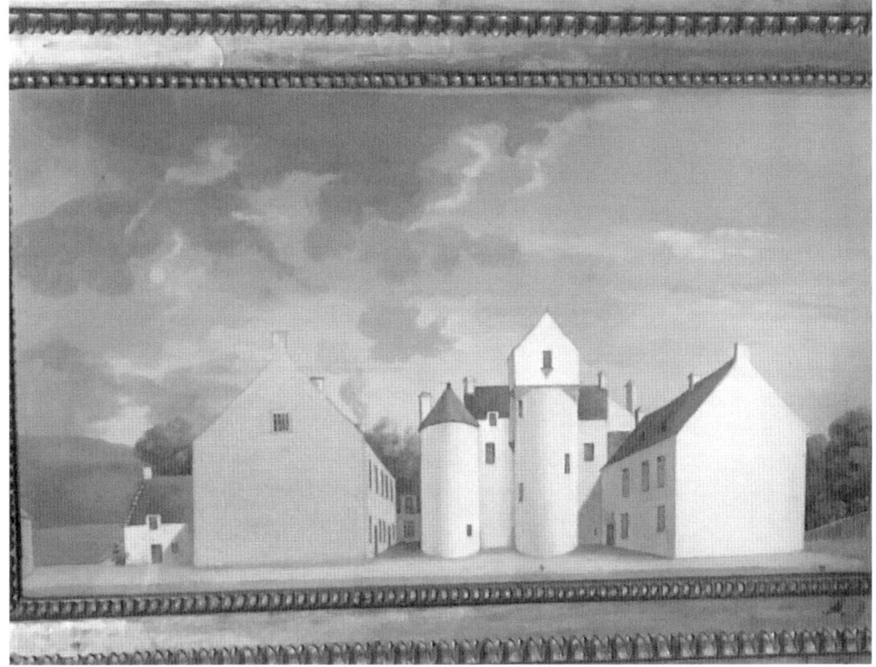

This historic watercolor shows a wing that James Grant added to Ballindaloch Castle while he was the Laird (*at the left*). *Courtesy of the Laird Guy Macpherson-Grant.*

During the Bartrams' visit, a somewhat less traditional dish would be included on Grant's menu: rattlesnake. This addition was the result of William Bartram's energy and agility, though it would also cause the young adventurer some personal regret.

The Bartrams arrived in St. Augustine in October 1765, but they had suffered a serious setback along the way, as John had come down with malaria. After a month of recuperation, he felt well enough to join a diplomatic meeting that Governor Grant and his administration held with the Creek Nation. William also attended, and the meeting took place near the banks of the St. John's River. While there, William and his father naturally took the opportunity to explore the countryside. As they were hiking a nearby trail, they spotted an enormous rattlesnake at their feet. The snake was more than six feet long, and William was understandably startled. Springing quickly into action, he cut a nearby sapling and used it as a club, dispatching the rattler with a single blow.

William later recalled how he fastened a vine around the neck of a snake and brought the body back to the camp: "I dragged him after me, his

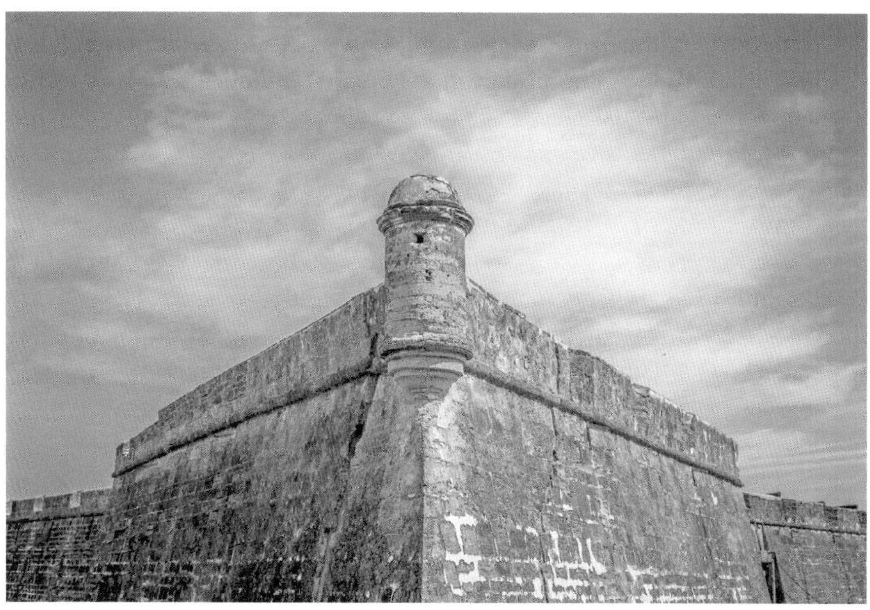

Castillo de San Marcos in St. Augustine was known as Fort St. Marks during the British period. *NPS photo, public domain.*

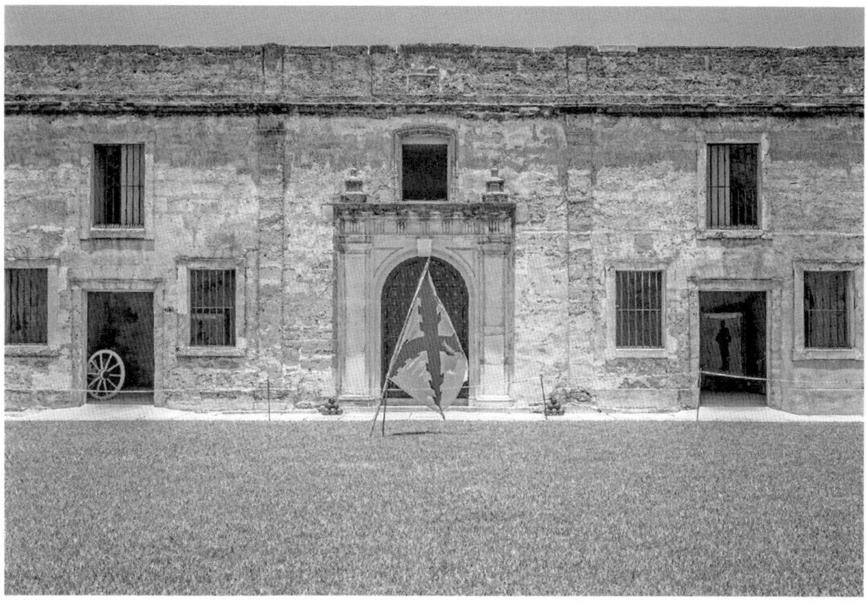

St. Augustine was the capital of British East Florida and a place of hospitality and support for the Bartrams. *NPS photo, public domain.*

scaly body sounding over the ground, and entering the camp with him in triumph, was soon surrounded by the amazed multitude, both Indians and my countrymen." He gave the snake to the cooks, and later that day, when William was invited to dine at the governor's table, he found that Grant was enjoying a dish of rattlesnake, which must have seemed exotic fare to the Scottish gourmet. William tried some himself, but without enthusiasm. "I tasted of it but could not swallow it," he recalled.

Regardless of the flavor of rattlesnake, guilt might also have affected William's appetite. In a characteristically conscientious reaction, he was beginning to feel remorse for having killed the snake, despite the deed being so applauded in the camp. He realized that dangerous though its venom was, the snake had not actually attacked him; he even came to believe that the snake had chosen not to strike at him, only to meet with a lack of any corresponding mercy from the human it had spared. This introspective and self-critical reaction from a young man who had just received public acclaim is a tell card for Bartram. It reflects the sincerity and thoughtfulness that would be central to his character throughout his life.

The Royal Botanist and Dr. Stork

After a further period of recuperation for John, who was still struggling with the aftereffects of malaria, the Bartrams set forth to explore the St. John's River. They traveled by dugout canoe, a vessel fashioned from an enormous log of cypress wood. The river journey alone would cover some five hundred miles.

The record of this journey was written by John rather than William. The result is that what must have been an adventurous trip is known mostly through a prosaic summation. The quality of soil at numerous points along the river is duly noted, and an inventory is provided of trees and plants. John's writing abounds in precise measurements, but it lacks the artistic and literary appeal that his son's later work would provide.

John's writing does represent a conscientious commitment to his responsibilities as royal botanist; the information he recorded would have been of pragmatic value for agricultural pursuits in the colony. As a result, John's report was reprinted in a very curious book published in 1766—a book that stands as an early example of a deliberate attempt to promote Florida development. The book was *A Description of East-Florida*, by Dr. William Stork.

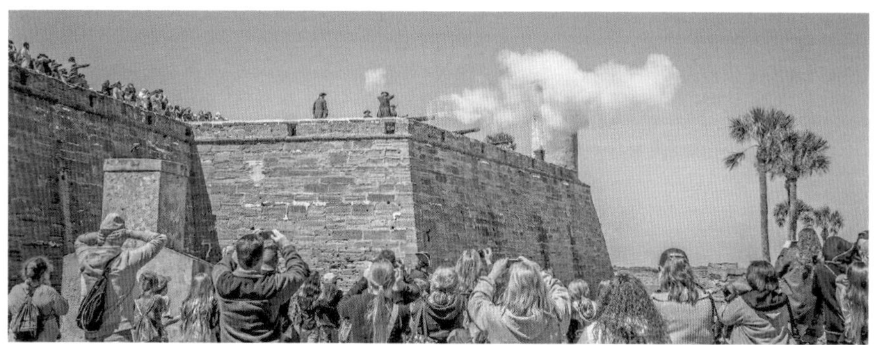

Cannon fire atop Castillo de San Marcos helps visitors imagine the swashbuckling days of colonial rivalries and intrigue. *NPS photo, public domain.*

Dr. Stork was an optometrist, author and traveler. At one point in his life, he is thought to have practiced in London while promoting his services, with the claim that he was the optometrist to the prince of Wales. Dr. Stork later traveled across the Atlantic to Philadelphia and then south to British Florida. His book about Florida painted a glowing picture of the agricultural and strategic potential of this newest North American holding.

Strategic potential? From Dr. Stork's viewpoint, Florida was indeed a strategic location, ideal for the British "to carry on a beneficial commerce with the Spanish settlements in time of peace; and to intercept, and cut off their trade in time of war." He wrote with a Machiavellian perspective on how quickly peace could turn to war and how profit could be made in either case. "As to the situation of Florida, with a view to surprize the Spanish ships in time of war, the trade winds oblige the register ships and galleons from Carthagena, Porto Bello, and Vera Cruz, the rich cargoes whereof are very well known, to return to Europe through the gulph of Florida, and to call at the port of the Havannah, in their way to Old Spain."

The second edition of Dr. Stork's book includes John Bartram's journal, duly attributed to its author. (The full title of the book's second edition was *A Description of East-Florida, with a Journal Kept by John Bartram of Philadelphia, Botanist to His Majesty for the Floridas; upon a Journey from St. Augustine up the River to St. John's as Far as the Lakes*. As in Catesby's time, this was still the age of long titles.) Dr. Stork valued Bartram's writings as providing scientific corroboration for his depiction of Florida's rich agricultural promise.

During this period of history, Florida was a sizable British territory with a very limited number of British citizens. Dr. Stork's book was intended to promote emigration. Regarding Florida, he wrote, "I foresee that its climate

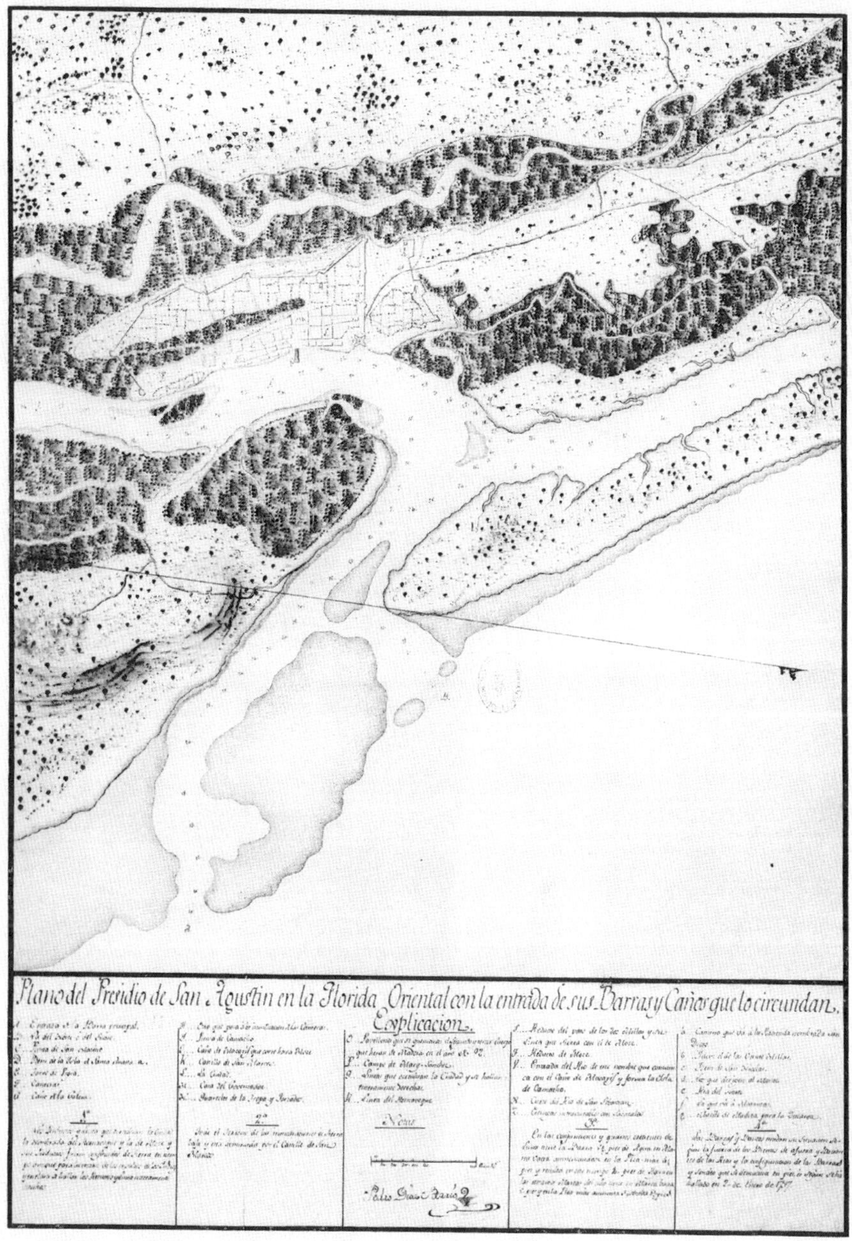

A map of St. Augustine in 1797—in between the visits of William Bartram and John James Audubon. *NPS photo, public domain.*

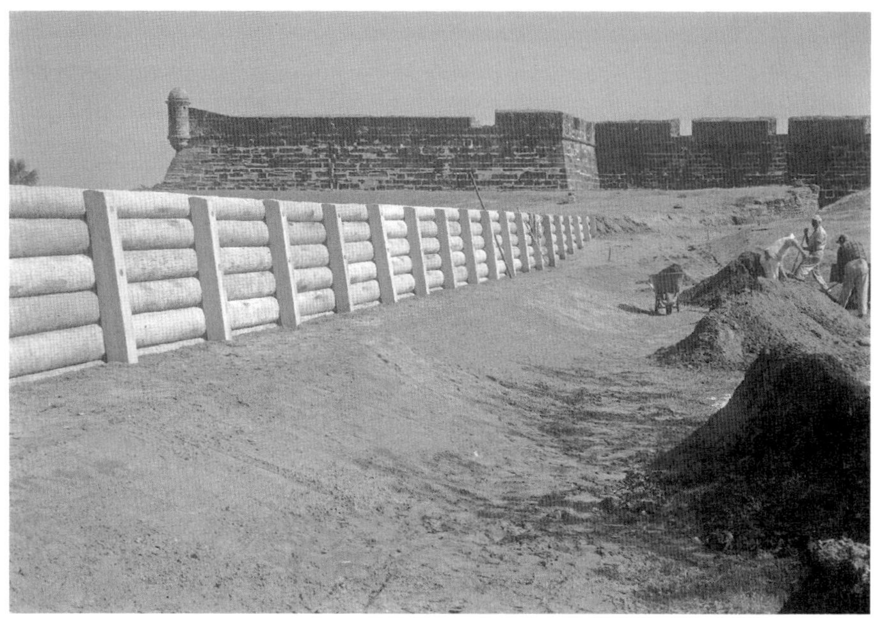

A reconstruction of a defensive wall at St. Augustine, also from the period between the visits of Bartram and Audubon. *NPS photo, public domain.*

and produce, as well as its situation, which, with respect to the Spanish dominions, is of great moment, will one day render it a very important colony to Great Britain; yet, the town of St. Augustine excepted, this country is at present, for want of inhabitants, little better than a desert."

Dr. Stork's great expectations were not to be realized. From the British perspective, Florida would remain a virtual wilderness until it was traded away at yet another negotiating table in Paris. That would be in 1783, following the American Revolution. Under the terms of the treaty signed then, Spain regained Florida, and in exchange, the Bahamas became part of the British Empire.

However, during the time that Florida was under British rule, William Bartram would return, traveling alone. These travels would take place mainly from 1774 to 1775. Florida was still very much "in a state of nature," as Governor Grant had described it. Bartram would chronicle this journey in his extraordinary and poetic book, *Travels*, and in his sketches. The sketches include images of alligators, turtles, sandhill cranes and other Florida creatures; accurate and closely observed botanical images; and respectful portraits of Native American chieftains.

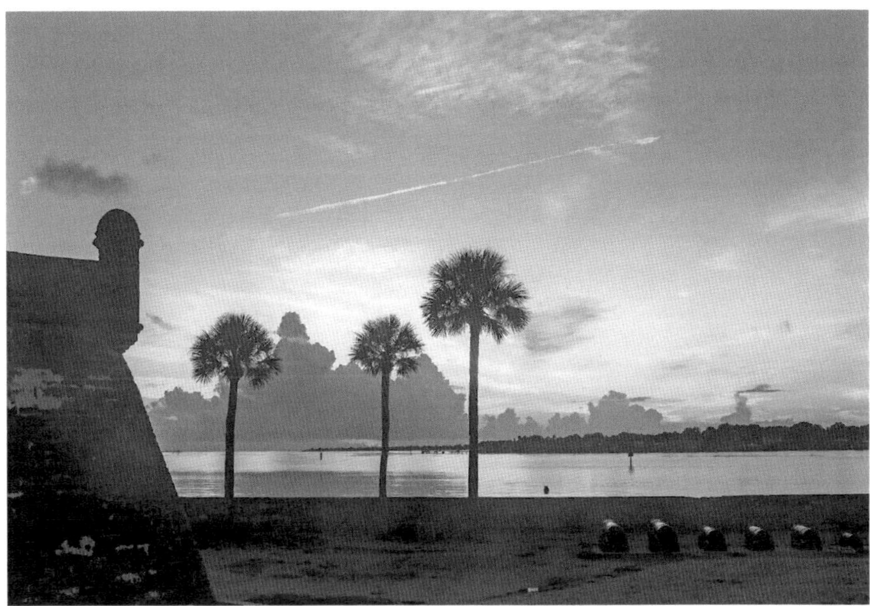

Sunrise at the Castillo. *NPS photo, public domain.*

The following chapters will explore William Bartram's writings and artwork. The purpose of these chapters is not to present a chronological reconstruction of his wanderings in Florida—a largely linear account is after all available in Bartram's book itself (*Travels*, Parts I and II). Instead, this is an invitation to adventure with Bartram, as highlights from his journey will be presented with a focus on their importance to natural history and art in Florida.

6

CROSSING THE LAKE OF ALLIGATORS

The most widely read passage from Bartram's *Travels* has always been the adventure with the alligators. It is a swashbuckling account of one of Florida's most iconic, and dangerous, creatures. And it has sparked questions that have been debated ever since.

Bartram's description of alligators sounds fabulous—maybe too fabulous. Was Bartram mixing fact and fiction? Eighteenth-century readers in the Northeast and Europe, who had never seen alligators, inevitably wondered about that. Readers in our time have wondered about it as well; familiar though we are with these living dinosaurs, some of Bartram's observations still seem dubious. Along with being the most famous chapter in Bartram's writing, it is also the chapter for which his accuracy has been the most frequently challenged.

Bartram also did a sketch of alligators, using his artistic skills to portray the exotic creatures. At first glance, the sketch might seem to only add to the doubts about his accuracy. It portrays two alligators in the St. John's River, and while Bartram realistically shows the appearance of the scaly bodies and tails, he is far less naturalistic in his drawing of the face and the snout. The eyes, in particular, seem to have a curiously mammalian appearance. There appear to be plumes of smoke rising from the nostrils of the creatures. Despite the carefully sketched plants and rock formations of the riverbank, the alligators themselves look as if they would be right at home on a mediaeval map under the heading "Here Be Monsters."

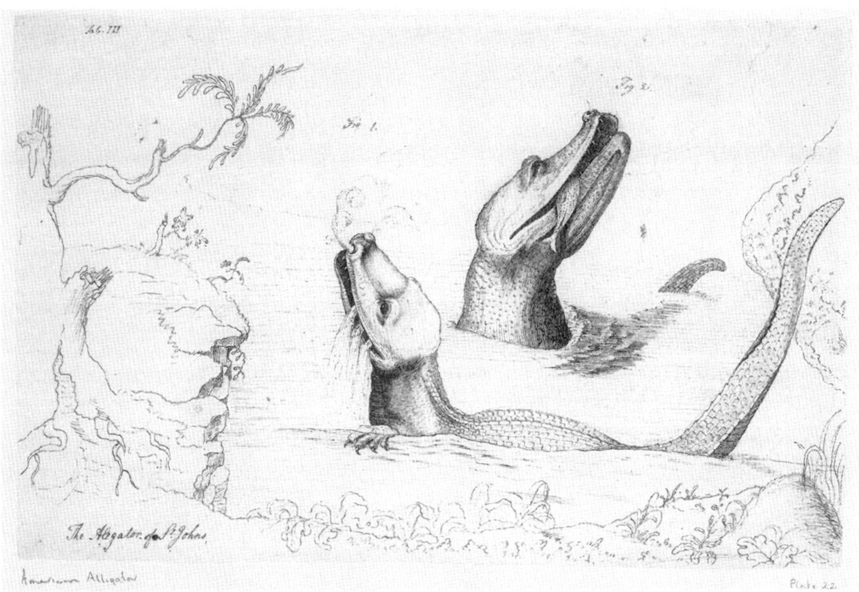

William Bartram's illustration of the alligators of the St. John's River. What appears to be smoke issuing from their nostrils is actually intended as vapor. *Courtesy of the Roving Naturalists, P.K. Yonge Library of Florida History, Special and Area Studies Collections, George A. Smathers Libraries, University of Florida, Gainesville, Florida.*

The alligator scenes in Bartram's *Travels* are as exciting as any storyteller could invent. Nevertheless, Bartram was a skillful observer of nature as well as an adventurer, and in fact, both of these character traits are apparent in his portrayal of Florida alligators.

The Battle

During the course of his explorations, Bartram had been traveling along the St. John's River by canoe. The river flowed into a lake known today as Lake Dexter; Bartram would call the area Battle Lagoon. It is not, technically, a lagoon, but it did prove to be a scene of battle. Before relating the danger that he himself was in, Bartram gives readers a dramatic account of a duel between two alligators, to which he was an eyewitness.

He begins his description of the duel by inviting us to imagine the deceptively peaceful area where it took place. The lakeshore was a place lush with vegetation, home to waterfowl such as coot and teal and fish such as trout. Suddenly, an alligator emerges from the reeds along the shore. Let Bartram himself describe what follows:

"His plaited tail brandished high, floats upon the lake. The waters like a cataract descend from his opening jaws. Clouds of smoke issue from his dilated nostrils. The earth trembles with his thunder. When immediately from the opposite coast of the lagoon, emerges from the deep his rival champion. They suddenly dart upon each other. The boiling surface of the lake marks their rapid course, and a terrific conflict commences." The alligators plunge beneath the water together, locked in combat.

Bartram continues, "The water becomes thick and discoloured. Again they rise, their jaws clap together, re-echoing through the deep surrounding forests. Again they sink, when the contest ends at the muddy bottom of the lake, and the vanquished makes a hazardous escape, hiding himself in the muddy turbulent sedge on a distant shore. The proud victor returns to the place of action. The shores and forests resound his dreadful roar."

How did Bartram, a solitary traveler in a canoe, feel at witnessing this spectacle? Understandably, he was nervous. He now knew that what had seemed an idyllic tropical waterway was home to these enormous and dangerous reptiles. The sun was sinking toward the horizon. What was he to do? Make camp? That offered scant hope of safety. "The alligators gathered around my harbour from all quarters." He decided to press onward in his canoe, continuing to brave the alligator-infested waters.

Bartram did give thought to finding a weapon to protect himself, and he made a curious choice: a piece of wood that he planned to use as a club. Although he had a gun—which would later play a role in his defense—he was afraid that if he tried to use it while in the canoe, he might accidentally drop it in the water. Perhaps he was also concerned that its retort might overset the balance of the canoe, plunging him into the water with the alligators, and he may have reasoned that the time required to reload the weapon would make it useless against so many foes. Thus, he settled on the bold idea of defending himself with a piece of wood. Modern readers might be reminded of Sir David Attenborough standing in the midst of Komodo dragons while holding a stick for self-defense in case the enormous reptiles became aggressive (a memorable scene from the *Living Planet* documentary series of the 1980s). Unlike Sir David, however, Bartram would actually have to make use of his improvised staff.

At first, the alligators gave way before the canoe, but soon, he was "attacked on all sides." He believed that the reptiles were trying to overturn his vessel. "My situation now became precarious to the last degree: two very large ones attacked me closely, at the same instant."

Yet fear not, dear reader, our intrepid naturalist is holding a piece of wood. "I applied my weapons so effectually about me, though at random, that I was successful to beat them off a little; when finding that they designed to renew the battle, I made for the shore, as the only means left me for my preservation; for, by keeping close to it, I should have my enemies on one side of me only, whereas I was before surrounded by them." Boldness and strategy won the day, and once Bartram reached the shore, the alligators ceased pursuing him. He naïvely thought this was because he would have been able to outrun them by land.

Next, Bartram had to decide whether to continue on land, which he thought would provide more immediate safety but would also mean abandoning his canoe. Recognizing that without a boat he would likely perish sooner or later in a trackless wilderness, he shrewdly opted to paddle along the shoreline as he continued his journey. This way, he would have the option of choosing either land or water as a place to make his stand in the face of future attacks.

At first, Bartram was able to continue his voyage quietly; he saw many alligators, but he was no longer pursued by them. However, he made the dubious decision to catch some fish for supper, and when he made camp

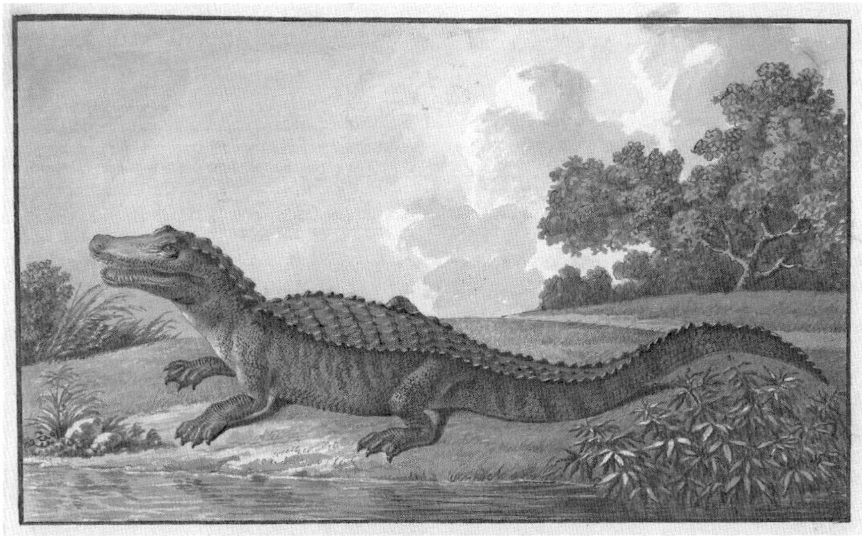

Bartram's illustration of an alligator on the shore. *Courtesy of the American Philosophical Society.*

for the night, he realized that he was being followed by a twelve-foot-long alligator. Now faced with a single foe, albeit one of massive size, Bartram laid aside his club in favor of his gun: "I soon dispatched him."

With considerable sangfroid, our traveler returned to his fish—but soon, yet another alligator appeared. "I saw before me, through the clear water, the head and shoulders of a very large alligator, moving slowly towards me. I instantly stepped back." This time, however, Bartram was in no danger more serious than that of losing his supper. "With a sweep of his tail, he brushed off several of my fish." Then, the giant alligator returned to the waters.

Bartram took this opportunity to reload his gun and reconnoiter the area around his campsite. Although he spotted numerous alligators in the waters nearby, he was reassured to see them feeding on an abundant supply of fish. He reasoned that they would have no need to seek out a human meal and settled into his campsite. With an admirable stiff upper lip, he relates how he found oranges growing on a nearby tree and used the fresh juice as a seasoning for his remaining fish. It is a high level of attention to culinary detail for a solitary traveler who had, not long before, used a piece of wood to drive alligators away from his canoe.

SURPRISING ACCURACY

It is easy to see why this account has sparked both excitement and skepticism ever since it was first published. It is the opinion of this author (that is, the author of the book you are now reading) that Bartram's story was exaggerated, but not intentionally so. Consider the matter from his perspective, taking the observer effect, so to speak, into account.

It is reasonable to suppose that if a large number of alligators were actually trying to attack a lone man in a canoe, the outcome would not be a happy one. In that instance, very few people today would ever have heard of William Bartram.

However, imagine yourself in a small canoe with alligators nearby. Do you think you might be somewhat intimidated? It is very understandable that Bartram felt frightened. How aggressive would the alligators really have to be before he *thought* he was under attack and in a panic began flailing about with his stick?

The incident from the campsite, when an alligator stole his fish, is also telling in this regard; so are Bartram's observations of the numerous alligators feeding on fish nearby. Alligators were abundant here because it was a rich fishing ground—not because they were hoping to eat a wandering Philadelphian. Thus, the alligators might have surrounded Bartram's canoe without having much interest in Bartram himself. In fact, it is quite possible that his impulse to thwack at the creatures with a piece of wood put him in more danger rather than less danger. Bartram's actions and even his perceptions of the incident show a very human combination of courage and panic.

As to his descriptions of the alligators themselves, it has been convincingly argued that they show a greater fidelity to accurate observation than meets the eye. Bartram was a thoughtful natural historian even when he believed himself in peril. Professor F. Wayne King, emeritus curator of the Division of Herpetology at the Florida Museum of Natural History in Gainesville, has written a monograph titled "Alligator Behavior: The Accuracy of William Bartram's Observations." King states: "Many writers have criticized Bartram's accounts as exaggerated, overly colorful fiction. Bartram was human and entirely capable of making mistakes, but his reports on American alligators contain relatively few errors and the ones that are present are easily explained misinterpretations of the facts."

For example, there is this famous (or perhaps infamous) line from Bartram's description of an alligator preparing to battle a rival: "Clouds of smoke issue from his dilated nostrils." At first glance, it seems to be a clearly fictitious, and even mythical, touch. However, the meaning of many words has changed since the late eighteenth century, and we must consider what Bartram may have meant by "smoke." King notes this usage: "The word 'smoke' is often used to refer to something that obscures, e.g., the convection fog that is known as Arctic sea smoke, or the humid mist that gave the name to the Great Smoky Mountains." Thus, King reasons that Bartram was describing water vapor, which could indeed issue from the dilated nostrils of an alligator that has just surfaced.

Not only is this a reasonable suggestion, but Bartram's sketch of alligators provides evidence that proves it. At first glance, the sketch may seem to show plumes of smoke, but Bartram labeled the image as "Figure 1" and provided a caption; the caption refers to "steam or *vapour* from their nostrils *like smoke*" (italics mine). Bartram was not portraying the alligator as a mythical monster; he was using the language of his time to describe a simple and natural phenomenon.

Then there is the matter of the cooperative feeding. Bartram observed this at the point where the St. John's River entered Lake Dexter. Large numbers of fish were passing into the lake at that point, and alligators were congregating there to feed. Bartram was surprised to see this at first, and then he breathed a sigh of relief, because this was the point when he realized the creatures were more interested in pursuing fish than they were in pursuing him. Though he escaped pursuit by the alligators, Bartram has been relentlessly pursued by critics with respect to this very passage and the question of whether alligators actually show such cooperative feeding behavior. Their skepticism is understandable; we are not talking about dolphins, after all. However, there is some evidence to support Bartram's assertions.

First of all, it is illuminating to consider a description of this behavior that Bartram gave in a letter; it is less poetic than the *Travels*, but on the other hand, it is a clearer and simpler explanation: "The Trout pass here in their way to & from the numerous lakes & endless Lagoons & Marshes towards the head of this Vast River, where they go to spawn. The Alegator post themselves forming a line.…We see them opening their voracious Jaws into which the fish are intrap't." Is that really so farfetched? With an abundance of fish available at that point, this strategy would be attributable to pure instinct and would not require the intellect of dolphins to devise.

Furthermore, corroboration is provided by observations of other crocodilians. In his monograph, Professor King points out that not only has cooperative feeding behavior been noted by other observers of the American alligator, but such behavior is also exhibited by the Yacare caiman in Brazil and by crocodiles in various regions of Africa. Interestingly, many of these supporting observations were made during the late twentieth century. It seems that Bartram was correct in his description of alligators feeding together on an abundance of fish; it just took two hundred years or so for his accuracy to be recognized.

Bartram provides information about alligator nests, but here he makes a definite error, considerably overestimating the number of eggs that a single nest contains. He believed that it was common to have one to two hundred eggs in a single nest; a more accurate count is twenty to fifty. When it comes to alligator parenting habits, however, Bartram provides information that is remarkably on point.

Since Bartram's account undeniably emphasizes the danger he was in when surrounded by alligators, it might be surprising that he nevertheless portrays the females as caring mothers. Following his discussion of the nests, he explains that even after the eggs have hatched, the young are not left to fend for themselves. He provides this touching imagery: "I have had frequent opportunities of seeing the female alligator leading about the shores her train of young ones, just as a hen does her brood of chickens; and she is equally assiduous and courageous in defending the young, which are under her care, and providing for their subsistence; and when she is basking upon the warm banks, with her brood around her, you may hear the young ones continually whining and barking like young puppies."

Such a characterization of maternal instinct from a cold-blooded reptile was another claim that provoked considerable doubt. However, the facts clearly prove that Bartram was right about this. When they are newly hatched, the young ones are actually carried in the mother's mouth, very gently, to the water. They will spend at least a year or two with their mother, enjoying her protection and her care.

All considered, the descriptions of alligators and their behavior seem to fit with this principled assessment of Bartram's work and legacy from the great Florida herpetologist Archie Carr: "Long ago…I decided that looking for fabrication in Bartram's reportage is unrewarding. Once in awhile he misinterpreted, but he almost never misobserved."

Adventurer, Storyteller, Observer

The crossing of the lake of alligators is the most famous passage in Bartram's *Travels*, and with good reason. It's like a chapter from an adventure novel—an adventure novel written by a very eccentric author. A heroic Quaker explorer uses a makeshift club to defend his canoe from giant reptiles; it could pass for an idea that Robert Louis Stevenson smiled at but laid aside, opting to write about pirates instead.

Yet along with establishing him as both an adventurer and a flamboyant storyteller, the chapter also shows William Bartram as a naturalist. He grew up in a garden, he sketched birds and trees as a youth, he traveled with his royal botanist father as a young man; now, he was exploring the Florida wilderness. He was understandably frightened by the dangerous creatures he encountered, yet nevertheless, he remained as curious as ever. It is as if his sketchpad and his journal were clutched in one hand even while his other hand kept a tight grip on the improvised club.

For William Bartram was always a naturalist, whether he was fighting for his life on a marshy lakeshore or tending a bed of tulips in a peaceful garden. Thus, his observations of alligators, despite being made under such perilous conditions, have proven to be perceptive and insightful.

7

THE FLOWER HUNTER

Bartram and the Seminole

During his travels, William Bartram had considerable contact with Native American societies, including the Florida Seminole, and his admiration for them is an important aspect of his work. As an artist, he sketched a Seminole chieftain, portraying him with great dignity. As a writer, he included extensive passages in his book describing Native customs; he also eloquently defended the virtues and honor of Native peoples.

To the modern reader, it may seem curious to find so much material about culture in a book written by a man who was primarily a botanist and natural historian. However, this would not have seemed strange in the eighteenth century. For one thing, Bartram's book is about his travels, as its title clearly indicates. Encounters with Native American societies were part of those travels. In fact, they are mentioned directly in the full title, which sounds lengthy even by eighteenth-century standards: *Travels Through North & South Carolina, Georgia, East & West Florida, the Cherokee Country, the Extensive Territories of the Muscogulges, or Creek Confederacy, and the Country of the Chactaws, Containing an Account of the Soil and Natural Productions of Those Regions, Together with Observations on the Manners of the Indians.* (It is no wonder that the book is today known simply as Bartram's *Travels.*)

Another reason why Bartram was so comfortable in combining cultural studies with nature studies is that the modern concept of specialization had not yet taken hold. Just as in the fifteenth and sixteenth centuries, Renaissance men like Leonardo da Vinci would have laughed at the thought of a separation between the sciences and the humanities, so likewise, an eighteenth-century scholar such as Bartram was expected to be curious and observant regarding many different fields of study. And he certainly lived up to such expectations.

Bartram was indebted to many of the Native Americans he met for their help and protection during the course of his journey. He was even given the honor of a special name, one that might give us insight into the other side of the coin—that is, how the Natives that he met viewed him.

"Humane and Compassionate"

Early in *Travels*, Bartram describes an encounter with a lone Seminole brave. The story proves to be a foreshadowing of how Native peoples would be portrayed in the rest of the book.

Bartram was traveling a forest path when he was startled to suddenly see a Native brave on horseback—armed with a rifle—coming toward him. "I never before this was afraid at the sight of an Indian, but at this time, I must own that my spirits were very much agitated." Bartram tried to hide behind trees, but it was futile for a Pennsylvania Quaker to try to elude a Seminole in the woods of Florida. He soon realized this, said a prayer and "resolved to meet the dreaded foe with resolution and cheerful confidence."

As they stood face to face, alone in the wilderness, the Seminole seemed to be both wrathful and distrustful. He shifted his rifle and looked around him on all sides. Bartram stepped forward, held out a hand and greeted the Native American as "Brother." There was a moment of silence, broken only by the sounds of the forest. Then, the Seminole returned Bartram's handshake. They parted in peace, and the Seminole gave Bartram directions to the nearest trading post.

It is a powerful moment in the *Travels* and a touchstone for Bartram's relationships with Native peoples. He goes on to state that when he arrived at the trading post, he learned that the lone Seminole had been badly treated there the day before and had threatened that in retaliation he would kill the next white man he met. That man was Bartram, yet the Seminole had been moved by the Quaker's peaceful and brotherly manner and had spared his life.

With gratitude and empathy, Bartram imagined this internal monologue on the part of the brave: "White man, thou art my enemy, and thou and thy brethren may have killed mine; yet it may not be so, and even were that the case, thou art now alone, and in my power. Live; the Great Spirit forbids me to touch thy life; go to thy brethren, tell them thou sawest an Indian in the forests, who knew how to be humane and compassionate." If the Seminole brave had been less compassionate, or if Bartram had been less respectful, the naturalist's adventures would have ended almost before they began.

THE GIFTS OF AHAYA

Later in his travels, Bartram visited a beautiful area that he called the Great Alachua Savanna. Today, this area of central Florida, south of Gainesville, is Paynes Prairie Preserve State Park. While he was in this region, he enjoyed the hospitality of a famous Seminole chieftain named Ahaya. Bartram, like most white people, referred to this chieftain as "Cowkeeper" because of his great herds of cattle. The *Travels* features a fascinating description of their encounter.

The Seminole were a relatively new tribe at the time, an offshoot of the Creek Nation in Georgia and Alabama. They came to Florida in the early eighteenth century as a reaction to increasing European colonization, seeking to continue their traditional way of life while also adapting to a new, sometimes subtropical environment. Thus, the Seminole nation was born. Ahaya was an important chieftain among them. He chose to ally himself with the British and against the Spanish in the colonial rivalry over Florida. To that end, Ahaya had visited Bartram's old friend Governor Grant in St. Augustine, and the Scottish military gentleman made him a Great Medal Chief, formalizing this alliance.

Bartram describes the Seminole village of Cuscowilla as having houses and gardens, surrounded by plots where maize was grown and fields where the cattle grazed. He took favorable note of the cleanliness of the village and realized the good effect this would have on the health of the inhabitants. Ahaya's home was larger than the others and situated on a hill. Bartram and the other members of his party (at this point, he was no longer traveling alone) were led there and given a welcome that was both dignified and warm. "The chief, who is called Cowkeeper, attended by several ancient men, came out to us, and in a very free and sociable manner, shook our hands, or rather arms (a form of salutation peculiar to the American Indians) saying at the same time, 'You are come.'" Ahaya was a tall man, about sixty years old, with the bearing of a warrior. He had a nose like the beak of an eagle and eyes lively and full of fire. He invited the travelers into his home, the ceremonial pipe was passed about and diplomatic compliments were exchanged.

In this peaceful atmosphere, the purpose of Bartram's natural history expedition was explained to Ahaya. The Seminole chieftain was receptive and helpful, giving Bartram "unlimited permission to travel over the country." It is of interest that Bartram implicitly recognizes Ahaya's authority in this matter; of course, the chieftain's decree was also essential to his safety.

Banquets were also part of the hospitality of the village. Dishes included venison stewed in bear's oil, beef from the famous cattle herds, corn cakes, hominy and a drink of water mixed with honey, which Bartram found very refreshing.

The natural historian never forgot his meeting with Ahaya, the "Cowkeeper" and Great Medal Chieftain. Along with the permission to travel and the promise of friendship, Ahaya gave the wandering natural historian another gift: his special name. Bartram recalls the chief "saluting me by the name of PUC PUGGY, or the Flower hunter, recommending me to the friendship and protection of his people." There is a touch of humor in the name, though Bartram might not have realized it. The Native peoples must have excelled Bartram in many ways when it came to forest lore. Yet for them, such knowledge was the foundation of their way of life, and it served largely practical ends. What did Ahaya and his people make of a white man from a northern city trekking through the Florida wilderness out of curiosity, searching for any plants that were new to him regardless of whether they had food value, medicinal value or no obvious value at all? The name "Flower Hunter" suggests the timeless humor of the man who lives off the land looking at the nature enthusiast from the city.

THE LONG WARRIOR

As an artist, Bartram sketched a portrait of a Native American whom he said was named Mico-chlucco, or the Long Warrior. In the translated name, *Long* might mean *Tall*. The portrait is a striking work of art, and it was used as an opening illustration for his book. It shows a desire to record Native attire and accoutrements with great detail, as well as an artist's skill in portraying the individuality of the subject. Doubtless, it sparked the curiosity of eighteenth-century readers on both sides of the Atlantic.

Mico-chlucco is wearing a headband with a plume of curling feathers. He has a fur cape around his shoulders and ornamentation on his head and around his neck, and he holds an emblem of authority in each hand. One emblem is a tomahawk, which is disproportionately small; either it is purely a symbol rather than a weapon or else Bartram got the scale wrong. (The latter is quite possible, since the hand that holds it is also disproportionately small.) In his other hand, he has a kind of ornamental rod or scepter adorned with feathers. This is an element that we will return to in the following chapter, since it might bear on one of the greatest mysteries of Bartram's work.

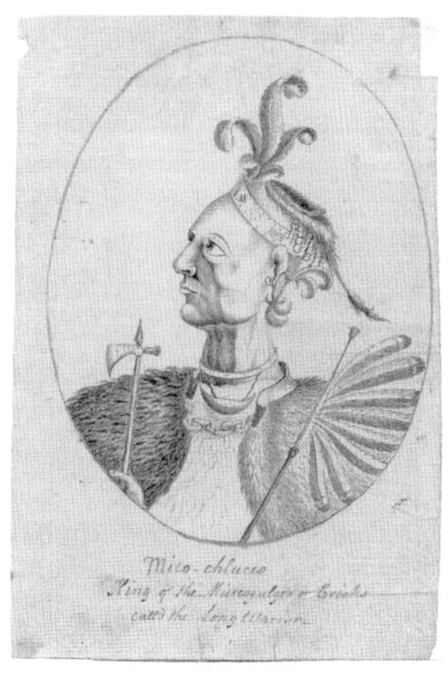

Bartram's portrait of the Seminole chieftain Mico-chlucco is a dignified image that shows the artist's interest in Native American cultures. *Courtesy of the American Philosophical Society.*

Regardless of any errors in scale, the portrait of Mico-chlucco reveals an undeniable artistry with texture. It is as if Bartram is trying to bring the sense of touch into the visual medium of the sketch. The fur cape looks rustic yet soft, and the feathers are so carefully delineated that the individual barbs are visible. Perhaps nowhere else in his work, save the finest of the botanical images, is Bartram's use of texture so skillful.

The face of Mico-chlucco, which is seen in profile, is upturned and is marked by an aquiline nose, high cheekbones and a broad forehead. The eyes are strikingly large, and here, the disproportion is likely deliberate; the size of the eyes and their upward gaze convey intelligence and sensitivity, with an implication of spirituality. In the eye that we can fully see (the portrait is a profile, after all), Bartram even depicts the reflection of light in the pupil and the luminous hues of the iris—challenging feats in a sketch. Furthermore, the use of shading on the upturned face shows Bartram's skill with the traditional artistic technique of chiaroscuro, the mixture of lights and shadows.

Who was this enigmatic figure, Mico-chlucco? He appears in Bartram's writing and is described as a martial chieftain of the Lower Creeks, that is, the Seminole. (Bartram uses the names "Creek" and "Seminole" somewhat interchangeably, a usage that accurately reflects the origins of the Seminole; he also uses "Muscogulges" as a third alternative name.) At the time that

Bartram met him, Mico-chlucco and forty of his men were on their way to wage war against the Chactaw tribe of western Florida. En route, they demanded supplies from an old trader named Charles McLatchie, of the St. John's River area. Bartram was a friend of McLatchie and was enjoying his hospitality at the time, so with the aid of an interpreter, he was able to witness and record an extraordinary interview between the Seminole chieftain and the riverside merchant.

Mico-chlucco demanded supplies on credit, stating that he and his warriors needed them for their impending campaign. McLatchie refused on the grounds that he was the agent of a mercantile company and would have to write to his superiors for their permission. At that, Mico-chlucco dramatically claimed that he could call thunder and lightning from the sky; the lightning would strike McLatchie down and burn his store to ashes.

The old trader kept his cool. He answered respectfully yet boldly that he knew Mico-chlucco was a renowned chieftain and a leader of valiant warriors, yet "he doubted if any man on earth had such power, but rather believed that thunder and lightning was under the direction of the Great Spirit." However, he invited the chieftain to display this power, if he could, by destroying a nearby oak tree.

The answer had the surprising effect of calming Mico-chlucco. The chieftain's reaction suggests he was neither as superstitious nor as arrogant as he may have seemed; he knew he was bluffing, and it was a bluff that the old trader had now called. Cleverly saving face, Mico-chlucco declared that in view of many previous acts of kindness from McLatchie, he would overlook this offense and not call down the lightning after all. McLatchie likewise stood his ground, answering that he was not frightened by lightning but that he did have great respect for Mico-chlucco and his people; thus, he suggested a compromise where he would give them half the supplies on credit, but they would have to pay on the barrel for the other half. This agreement seemed to please everyone, and the theatrical negotiations concluded in peace.

However, there was a strange epilogue to this that involved Bartram more personally. A large rattlesnake was seen in the Seminole camp, and three young braves, "richly dressed and ornamented," appealed to Bartram to kill it or drive it away. "Understanding that it was my pleasure to collect all their animals and other natural productions of their land, [they] desired that I would come with them and take him away, that I was welcome to him." The venomous rattlesnake was a specimen they would be happy to have the naturalist take off their hands, to be sure! Evidently, it was strongly against their traditions to kill a rattlesnake, so even the most valiant of their warriors would be unwilling to strike it down. For his own reasons, Bartram was reluctant to intervene; perhaps he recalled his feelings of guilt years before, when he had killed the rattlesnake that he thought had spared him. However, under the fervent entreaties of the Seminole, he gave in and "dispatched" the reptile for them. Then, carefully removing the venomous fangs, he placed the rest of the rattlesnake's remains in his collection of specimens.

Soon thereafter, the story took an unexpected turn. Bartram was suddenly accosted by two young braves bearing weapons. Why? Because he had killed the rattlesnake! Bartram must have been puzzled at being under attack for doing just what he had been asked to do. The braves declared that they would not kill him, but they would make him bleed. Then, another young Seminole, one who was held in high regard (Bartram calls him a "prince"), stepped forward to defend the naturalist and rattlesnake-killer. He declared that Bartram was "a brave warrior and his friend." At that, the others accepted his word and began shouting excitedly that the Flower Hunter was their friend.

When his initial confusion subsided, Bartram concluded that the incident was a kind of pantomime. Thanks to Bartram, the Seminole had been able to rid their camp of the dangerous reptile without breaking their customs, and the display of threatening to chastise him but then accepting him as their friend was evidently staged. It was an elaborate method of balancing safety and tradition.

The story is a vivid account of Bartram's efforts to navigate a culture that he respected but did not fully understand. It also provides intriguing background to his memorable portrait of Mico-chlucco, the Long Warrior.

"Honour and Reputation"

Along with such personal portraits and adventures, Bartram's work includes a thoughtful defense of Native American civilization. He appreciated the value that peoples such as the Seminole placed upon the "honour and reputation of their tribes and families." It is from this sense of honor, he wrote, that "their laws and customs receive force and energy."

Bartram believed that the Seminole provided "the most striking picture of happiness in this life; joy, contentment, love, and friendship, without guile or affectation, seems inherent in them, or predominant in their vital principle, for it leaves them but with the last breath of life." He speaks of the dignity of their elderly ones and the respect with which such experienced voices were listened to. He admired the ability of Native American peoples to live off the land and said that they had nothing to be anxious about except for "the gradual encroachments of the white people." To foster understanding and peace, he suggested that diplomats should learn the languages of the Native American tribes.

He also directly addressed the then-common portrayals of Native Americans as warlike, doing so in a realistic and shrewd way. Bartram acknowledged that tribes fought each other—his own encounter with Mico-chlucco had taken place as a result of intertribal war—but he cautioned his readers against hypocrisy. His perspective as a Quaker gave him insight here. The Quakers made a conscientious choice to follow a peaceful way of life, and doing so often required them to stand apart from other Europeans and colonials. In keeping with this viewpoint, Bartram noted that the motives for warfare among Native Americans "spring from the same erroneous source as they do in all other nations of mankind." As a thoughtful outsider to martial matters, he listed those motives: "The ambition of exhibiting to their fellows a superior character of personal and national valour, and thereby immortalizing themselves, by transmitting their names with honour and lustre to posterity; or revenge of their enemy, for public or personal insults, or, lastly, to extend the borders and boundaries of their territories." He knew that such motives would (or should) sound very familiar to many of his readers, and he was reminding them that these causes of warfare, and the resulting bloodshed, can be found in the histories of all nations.

Early in his travels, Bartram had preserved his own life with a gesture of peace toward a lone Seminole brave. Peacefulness and respect toward Native Americans continued to be themes in his journey and in his writing. This led him to find friends whose ways he did not fully understand but whom he accorded sincere respect. In turn, their hospitality and protection helped to ensure the success of his expedition and the survival of the Flower Hunter in the wilderness of Florida.

8

THE CASE OF THE MISSING VULTURE

"There is no more inviting nor singular problem in North American Ornithology." So wrote natural historian John Cassin in 1853. Cassin was using a phrase worthy of Sherlock Holmes before Sir Arthur Conan Doyle had even invented the great fictional detective, and he was describing a mystery that William Bartram left behind.

In his *Travels*, Bartram described three different types of vultures that he observed in eighteenth-century Florida. His description of the black vulture is important, because it is the first written account of the bird; Bartram is thus credited for the scientific discovery of the species. He also observed turkey vultures. Today, those are the only two species of vulture in Florida. Bartram, however, described a third species of vulture, a seemingly unmistakable creature with such flamboyant plumage that he called it the "painted vulture." No such creature is known to exist in Florida today. Nor was it observed by nineteenth-century visitors like John James Audubon. Thus, the identity of Bartram's painted vulture is the inviting and singular problem in question.

A Colorful Bird

Consider first the clues from Bartram's description. He begins by telling us that he is about to describe two vultures "not mentioned in history," that is, undiscovered in the scientific sense. One would be the black vulture, as

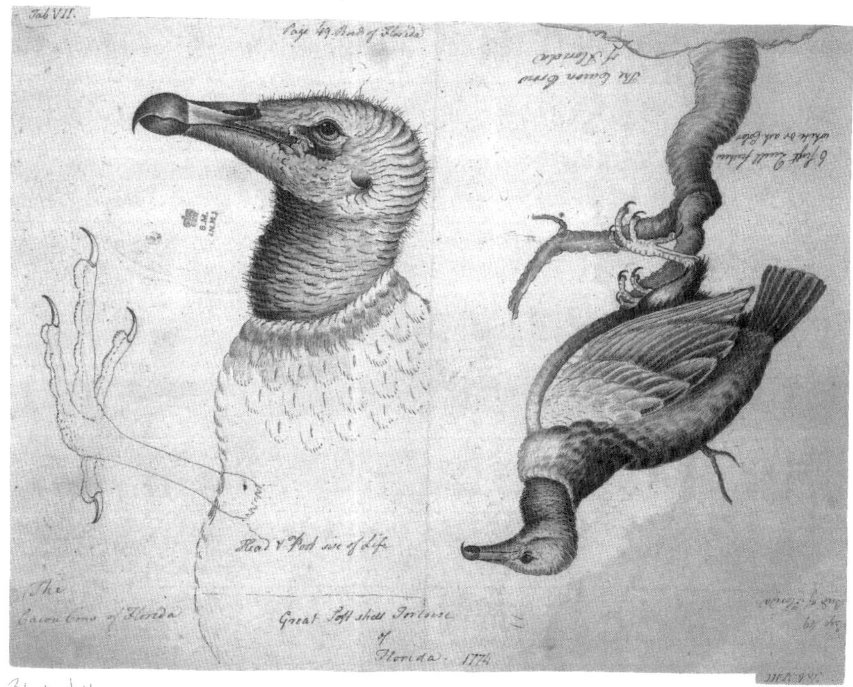

Bartram is credited with the first scientific description of the black vulture, which he illustrated here. He also described a colorful vulture that he called the "painted vulture," which is far more mysterious; unfortunately, there is no extant sketch by Bartram of that much-debated bird. *Courtesy of the Roving Naturalists, P.K. Yonge Library of Florida History, Special and Area Studies Collections, George A. Smathers Libraries, University of Florida, Gainesville, Florida.*

Bartram realized that he was the first to classify the species. The other is his painted vulture: "a beautiful bird," he called it.

A beautiful vulture? The bright colors of this bird did give it a kind of beauty. The neck was "a deep bright yellow colour intermixed with coral red." Colors of purple and orange were also noticeable, and the bird had a red crown. White, cream and brown were prominent in the coloring of the plumage, and the tail was white except for a tip of dark brown or black.

The controversy regarding this passage parallels that surrounding the alligator adventure. Some critics have dismissed the painted vulture as imaginary. Others have suggested that it was actually a caracara, which is only slightly less patronizing toward Bartram. The northern caracara is a bird that we will encounter in our consideration of Audubon's work in Florida; it is admittedly a carrion feeder, but it has a distinctive light blue beak and bears little resemblance to the description Bartram gives of his painted vulture.

The curator of Bartram's Garden in Philadelphia, Joel T. Fry, has, along with Noel F.R. Snyder, written a compelling defense of William Bartram's observations. The article is titled "Bartram's Painted Vulture: A Bird Deserving Recognition," and it advances a far more credible theory that would account for Bartram's observation. A variant theory, also eminently reasonable, was proposed by Francis Harper, a great Bartram scholar of the twentieth century and author of a valuable annotated edition of the *Travels*. Harper, in turn, had built on the work of nineteenth-century historians like Cassin (who had expressed such interest in the mystery).

These theories hinge on a connection to a bird that is very much alive today. The king vulture is found throughout much of South America, as well as Central America. Today, the northern limit of its range is Mexico; however, Bartram visited Florida two and a half centuries ago, and this bird may well have had a wider range then. Significantly, the king vulture has the bold colors of yellow, red, orange and purple that Bartram describes for the painted vulture. The combination of these unusual colors on a New World vulture makes it seem only reasonable that there is a correlation between the king vulture and Bartram's painted vulture.

Before we delve further into this conclusion and its implications, there is another line of evidence from Bartram's writings that must be considered. Perhaps surprisingly, this clue relates to the portrait of Mico-chlucco, the Long Warrior.

FEATHERS OF THE ROYAL STANDARD

Bartram notes that the tail feathers of the painted vulture were used by Native Americans in Florida for royal standards. Red paint was added to the feathers when they were to be carried into battle, whereas during peaceful negotiations, they were displayed "new, clean, and white." These standards were venerated and treasured.

In Bartram's portrait of Mico-chlucco, the warrior chieftain is holding a rod with feathers on it. Perhaps this is one of the royal standards that Bartram was referring to. There is no surviving illustration of the bird itself by Bartram, so his sketch of the feathers ornamenting Mico-chlucco's rod might be the closest thing we have. It is a far cry from a picture of the entire bird, but given the intrigue and controversy surrounding this aspect of Bartram's work, it has nevertheless attracted attention. See page 62.

Thus, Fry and Snyder describe the feathered rod that Mico-chlucco is holding as "a potential royal standard" and note that "as illustrated, the feathers visible in this portrait provide a reasonably close match to those he described" for the painted vulture. They add that the feathers "do not closely resemble any tail feathers" of the caracara, nor those of either bald eagles or golden eagles. "Thus, at least in this illustration he was apparently not confusing the tail feathers of these other species with the tail feathers of the painted vulture." So, the accoutrements of Mico-chlucco's portrait might give a tantalizing glimpse of Bartram's lost vulture species.

However, Francis Harper, while not doubting Bartram's veracity, nevertheless suggested that eagle feathers rather than vulture feathers were used in the royal standards. He noted that Bartram himself admits that the Native Americans referred to the feathers "by a name signifying eagle's tail." Harper thought it likely that the tail feathers of the juvenile golden eagle were used for the war standard, while the tail feathers of the bald eagle were used for the "new, clean, and white" peace standard. A complication with this part of the case is that although Bartram tells us that the feathers for the war standard were partly painted red by the Seminole, his sketch is monochromatic. Identification is definitely a challenge.

All in all, then, the feathers on Mico-chlucco's rod seem like an intriguing clue in the mystery of the painted vulture; however, this is a clue that leads us in a circle. The feathers may provide a trace of the painted vulture, but they do not really allow for identification of the species.

Thankfully, however, there is another lead in this case. For although Bartram's description of the painted vulture does not match any bird found in the wild in Florida, it bears a striking resemblance to a species that is recognized, and very much alive, today.

The Mystery Solved?

There is one unavoidable discrepancy between the description of the painted vulture and the appearance of the king vulture, and that is in the color of the tail. The king vulture has a black tail; Bartram describes the painted vulture as having a white tail merely tipped with black or dark brown. There is no phase in the king vulture's life when the tail color would match Bartram's description. However, the rest of the description matches well—even to the most florid colors and their unusual combination. As Sherlock Holmes might say, the odds are enormously against this being a coincidence.

As to the difference in the color of the tail, there are several possible explanations. Perhaps Bartram saw king vultures in Florida and described them with great accuracy, save for one mistake—the color of the tail. This was the view of Francis Harper. On the other hand, perhaps Bartram's painted vultures were a regional variation of the king vulture with a difference in coloring. This would make the painted vulture a subspecies of the king vulture or perhaps a closely related distinct species. These arguments are made by Fry and Snyder, with their preference being for the latter classification.

All of these theories presuppose that the population of these vultures in Florida became extinct at some point following Bartram's visit. After all, if you wish to see a king vulture today, you must visit a place like the Brevard Zoo. And since there have been no reported sightings of this bird in Florida by anyone other than Bartram—a fact that has added considerably to the intrigue surrounding his account—the extinction presumably took place much closer to his time than to ours.

It must be remembered Florida was very much a wilderness when Bartram was here and remained so for some time afterward. The next major expedition in Florida (especially in terms of ornithology) was, actually, that of our next artist—John James Audubon. And Audubon came some fifty years after Bartram. That half-century is the likely timeline for the extinction to have taken place; it is absurd to think that Audubon would have missed a bird as large and colorful as the painted vulture.

Why the bird would have become extinct in Florida is unknown, but then again, so is the size of the Florida population to begin with. Bartram describes them as gathering in the vicinity of fires to feed on reptiles that had been unable to escape from the blaze—familiar vulture behavior—but he does not necessarily indicate that the birds were numerous in Florida. The population might always have been small, dwindling and then vanishing sometime between the visits of Bartram and Audubon.

Questions remain, but it does seem clear that Bartram's lost painted vulture was connected to the still-living king vulture. Whether Bartram was observing a regional variation, a subspecies or a closely related species, his writings provide evidence that the exotic king vulture of Latin America had a counterpart in Florida during the eighteenth century. Thus the "inviting and singular problem" of the missing vulture has, at least, a partial solution—one that fits with the honesty of Bartram's character and his importance as a natural historian

9

"SILVER REGIONS OF THE CLOUDED SKIES"

Science and Artistry in Travels

After Bartram's journey in British East Florida came to an end, years would pass before the publication of the *Travels*. For one thing, the natural historian had not yet ended his wandering. He would continue his adventures with treks in Georgia and the Carolinas. He even returned to Florida—this time visiting British West Florida. However, a bout of illness interfered with this trip, and the passage in the *Travels* is correspondingly brief; it includes a detailed description of Pensacola (then the capital of British West Florida) but does not have the kind of importance to natural history that his earlier expedition did.

When he returned to Philadelphia, Bartram settled into the cloistered and peaceful world of the family gardens, and for the most part, he remained settled there for the rest of his life. This seems surprising for such an adventurer who was still only in his late thirties; however, the botanical gardens were an apt place to continue natural history research and maintain a varied correspondence. Besides, he had a great deal of writing to do.

It took considerable time for Bartram to write his book and arrange for publication. Such delays were inevitable given the kind of book that Bartram was working on, but they cost him something in terms of scientific credit, especially with the names of plants. Some species of plants that Bartram would have been credited with discovering were written about by other natural historians during the interim. When the *Travels* was finally published, it bore the date 1791. Bartram's primary Florida adventures had taken place in 1774 and 1775.

Nevertheless, the book was worth the wait. Bartram's *Travels* is an extraordinary combination of scientific achievement and artistry. The artistry is to be found not only in his engaging sketches but also in the poetic flair of his writing. This chapter will provide some final highlights from Bartram's work and a consideration of his eclectic circle of admirers.

THE CASTLES OF THE TORTOISES

Bartram was the first writer to describe an endearing Florida animal: the gopher tortoise. He is thus credited with its discovery. The ecological importance of the gopher tortoise, today recognized as a keystone species, underscores the importance of this feature of Bartram's work.

"This strange creature remains yet undescribed by historians and travelers," wrote Bartram of "the great land tortoise, called gopher." He thus knew that he was the scientific discoverer of the species, just as he knew that he was the scientific discoverer of the black vulture. The large size of the gopher tortoise was noted by Bartram; he also gave a description of the shell and mentioned their potentially camouflaged nature in field and forest.

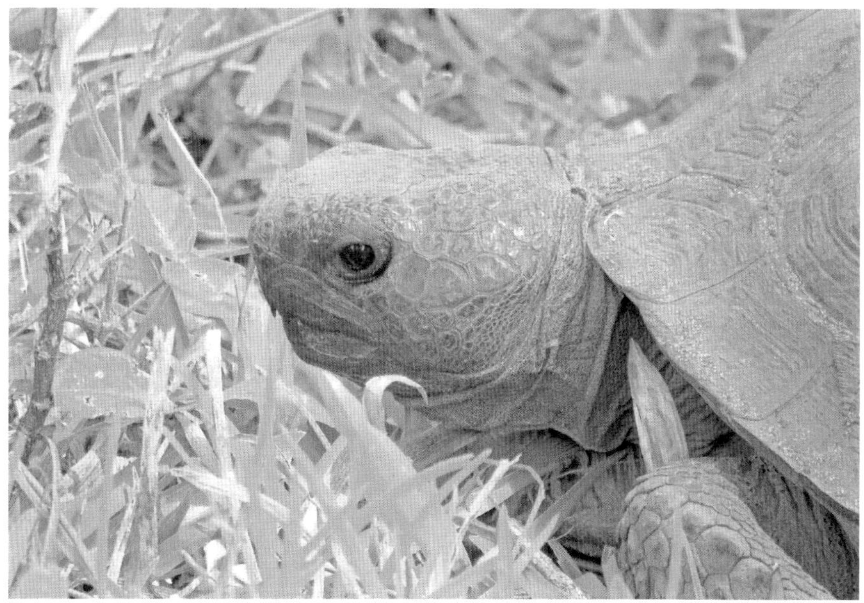

The gopher tortoise is an endearing Florida creature. Bartram accurately described the burrows made by the gopher tortoise. So many other animals benefit from the burrows that the gopher tortoise is today recognized as a keystone species. *Author's collection.*

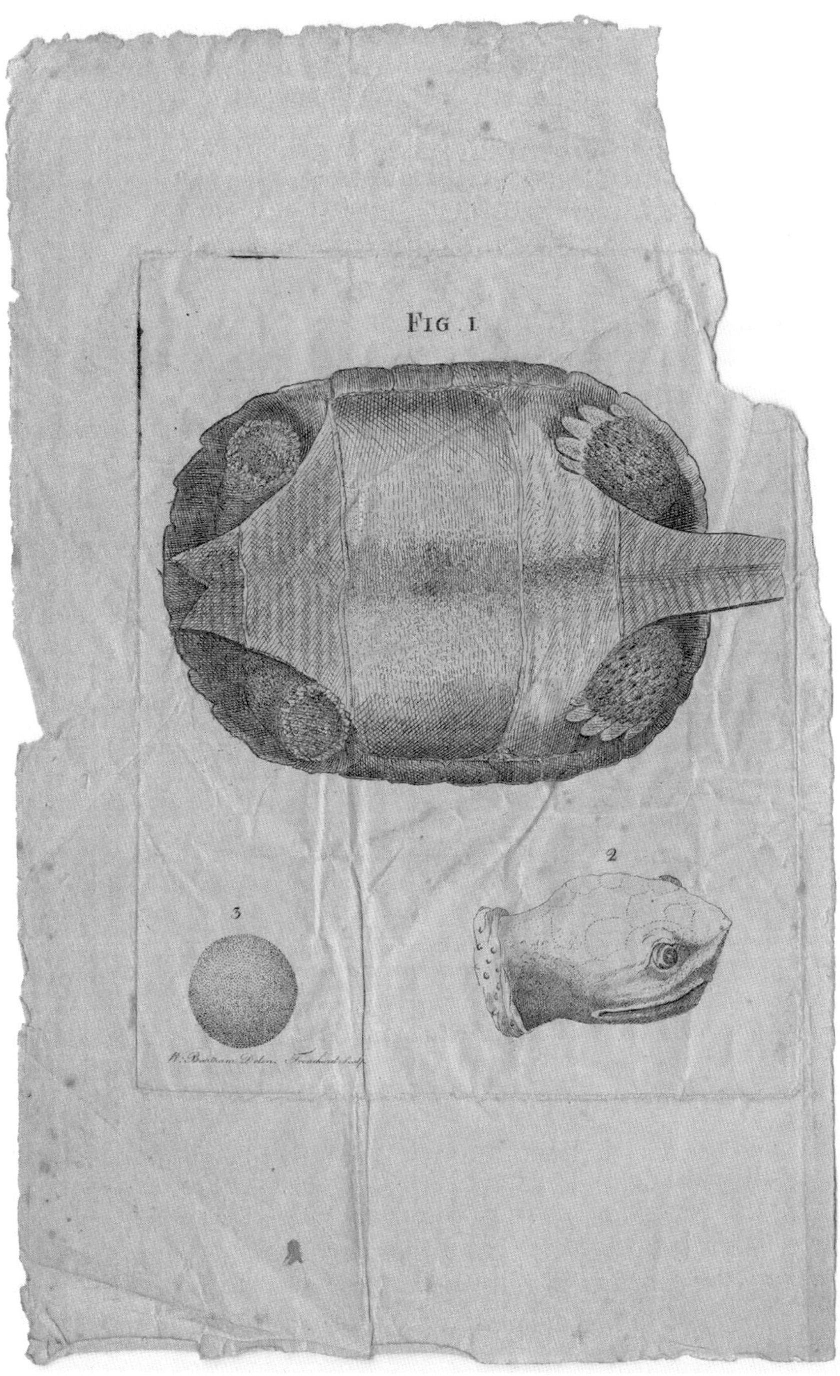

Bartram was the first writer to describe the gopher tortoise, and he made this scientific sketch of the animal. *Courtesy of the American Philosophical Society.*

Significantly, he also wrote about the burrows of these amazing creatures. The fact that so many other creatures make use of the burrows is what gives the gopher tortoises their keystone species title. Over three hundred species of vertebrates benefit indirectly from their work; the inclusion of insect species brings the count even higher. Bartram could not have known all of that, but he was certainly impressed by the scale on which the tortoises worked. "They form great and deep dens in the sand hills, casting out incredible quantities of earth," he wrote. He was correct. Burrows have been found that are more than fifty feet long, and some burrows are twenty feet deep. A gopher tortoise can dig nine feet of tunnel in a single day's work.

"These vast caves are their castles," Bartram wrote. He probably did not realize how true this poetic statement would prove to be. The end chamber of a gopher tortoise burrow has a dome shape that is strong and stable. Due to its proximity to the water table, it has just the right level of humidity for a tortoise's health and happiness. Each tortoise chooses a spot where the water table is sufficiently low so that the burrow will not be flooded after rainfall. They also make sure that the entryway is in a spot that will have direct sunlight for part of each day, so that they can enjoy basking. Just like castles, gopher tortoise burrows are marvels of engineering and architecture.

THE ART OF BOTANY

Not for nothing was Bartram given the name Flower Hunter. Botany was a major aspect of his work in natural history. This was an interest he and his father shared. Between them, John and William Bartram are credited with the scientific discovery of over two hundred North American plants. This number is even more extraordinary considering the fact that William's delay in publishing the findings of his expedition to Florida cost him some of his own claims. Yet even so, the father-son duo achieved this astonishing number of botanical discoveries. It is no wonder that Bartram's Gardens were so renowned.

Bartram's love of botany also inspired some of his artwork. His botanical sketches are numerous, and they show extensive range. Some are precise, linear and scientific, but others are clearly intended for beauty as well as study. These convey the loveliness of the flowers and foliage while sacrificing nothing of the scientific accuracy and value. In this category, among the most famous of the images is that of the plant that John and William discovered and named for family friend Ben Franklin.

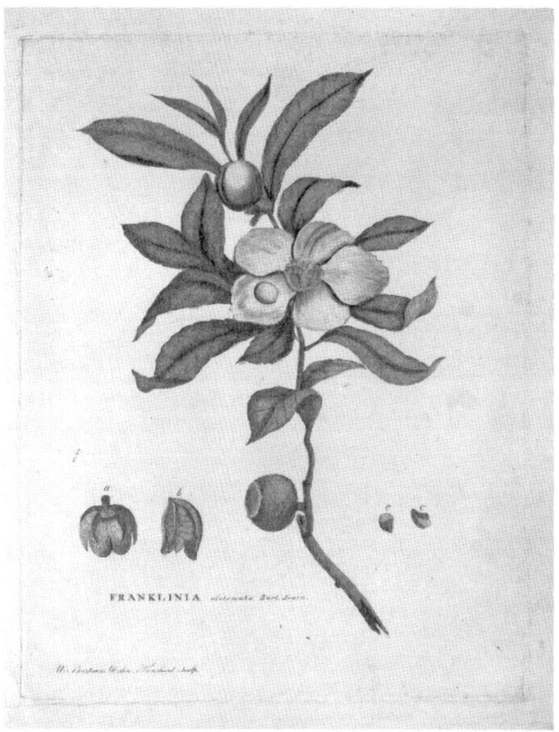

The Franklin Tree was discovered by the Bartrams and named for family friend Ben Franklin. William Bartram helped to preserve the species as well as beautifully illustrating it. *Courtesy of the American Philosophical Society.*

The Franklin Tree, *Franklinia alatamaha*, was discovered by the Bartrams in Georgia. Now extinct in the wild, it survives in gardens thanks to William, who brought some of its seeds back to the Bartram Gardens. Thus, William Bartram not only celebrated the tree with a work of art, but he also saved its species.

Franklinia alatamaha is, as William put it, "a flowering tree, of the first order of beauty and fragrance of blossoms." His illustration of it focuses on the flowers; instead of showing the entire tree, the composition is based on a sprig of blossoms. These blossoms are large and luxuriant, and their petals look as soft as velvet. Along with the portrait of Mico-chlucco, this is one of Bartram's masterpieces of texture; the apparent softness of the blossoms is contrasted by the brittle bark of the stem. The lines of the leaves are presented with almost microscopic detail. The connection with Ben Franklin adds to the interest of this work and its fame. The fact that the Bartrams not only discovered the species but also saved it gives another layer of meaning to a self-evidently lovely botanical illustration.

A colored sketch of a hibiscus from the St. John's River area provides an example of a distinctively Floridian flower as portrayed in William

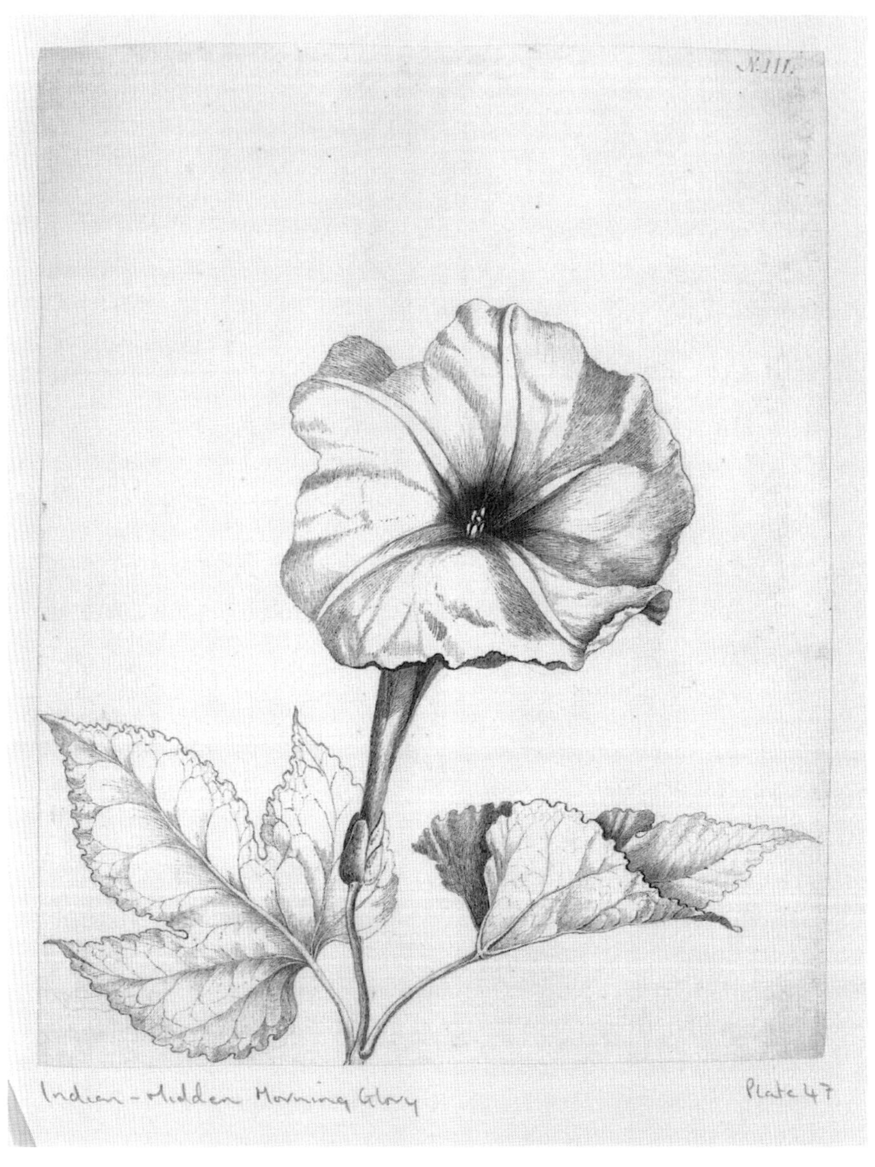

The morning glory was another subject for Bartram's botanical artwork. *Courtesy of the Roving Naturalists, P.K. Yonge Library of Florida History, Special and Area Studies Collections, George A. Smathers Libraries, University of Florida, Gainesville, Florida.*

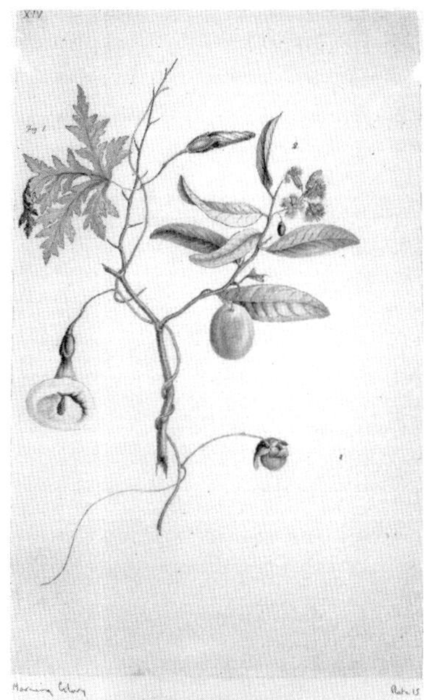

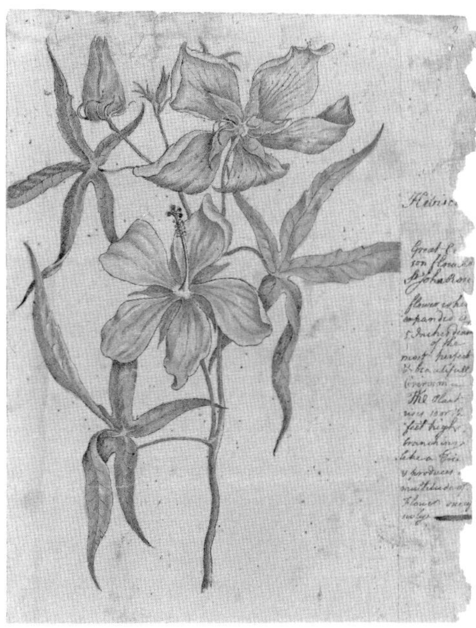

Left: Another image of the morning glory. *Courtesy of the Roving Naturalists, P.K. Yonge Library of Florida History, Special and Area Studies Collections, George A. Smathers Libraries, University of Florida, Gainesville, Florida.*

Right: This image of a hibiscus flower was likely a field sketch in Bartram's journal. *Courtesy of the American Philosophical Society.*

Bartram's artwork. The color sketch of the hibiscus is not so richly textured as the image of the Franklin Tree; however, it makes fine use of chiaroscuro, the traditional technique of realistically portraying light and shadow, which Bartram had also used with great effect in his portrait of Mico-chlucco, especially in the Native chieftain's face. With the hibiscus, Bartram employs chiaroscuro to provide realism and depth for both the petals and the leaves. The tall central pistil of the hibiscus flower, a distinctive feature, is clearly portrayed.

The simplicity of this image in comparison to the richness of the Franklin Tree illustration is understandable when one considers the fragment of text that appears to the right of the hibiscus. The text is cut off and it is evident that Bartram made this sketch on a notebook page; the torn page, with the picture, is the portion that has survived (and it is preserved today in the archives of the American Philosophical Society). Bartram's hibiscus was likely a field sketch done on site for his own reference. From that standpoint, it no longer seems simplistic but remarkably thorough. It is of great interest that Bartram took the trouble of using the chiaroscuro technique for a field sketch; this shows his love for art as well as for botany.

Hawkeye, the Ancient Mariner and George Washington

The *Travels* is a work of natural history, and it is also a work of literature. Thus, it attracted a varied crew of readers and admirers, both in Bartram's own day and in subsequent generations.

William Bartram's writing style is a rich reflection of eighteenth-century civilization. It abounds with metaphor and simile, classical allusions and biblical references. Bartram's Quaker background and his personal devotion give an undercurrent of spirituality to his writing; this is not separated from his study of nature but rather provides an intense motivation for it. He wrote this description of himself: "Continually impelled by a restless spirit of curiosity, in pursuit of new productions of nature, my chief happiness consisted in tracing and admiring the infinite power, majesty, and perfection of the great Almighty Creator." His accounts of the beauty of nature are seamlessly interwoven with expressions that evoke the Psalms of David. In his introduction, for example, he describes our planet and its place in the universe thusly: "This world, as a glorious apartment of the boundless palace of the sovereign Creator, is furnished with an infinite variety of animated scenes, inexpressibly beautiful and pleasing, equally free to the inspection and enjoyment of all his creatures." Bartram's portrayal of the Alachua Savanna is Edenic in nature, and it is a justly beloved passage of the *Travels*, which will furnish our concluding look at this artistic writer.

The poetic and spiritual aspects of Bartram's work, as well as the admiring portrayal of Native American cultures, would influence the classic American author James Fenimore Cooper. With his "Leatherstocking Tales," most famously *The Last of the Mohicans*, Cooper gave the world unforgettable characters whose lives are interwoven with nature: Natty Bumppo and his Mohican friends Chingachgook and Uncas. Natty Bumppo is a wise and profoundly honest man, a scout versed in every aspect of forest lore. He is usually known by names that have been given to him as descriptive of his attributes, such as Hawkeye and Pathfinder. This is very much in the Native tradition that gave William Bartram the name Flower Hunter. Furthermore, Hawkeye's earnest expressions of love for nature and God, as well as the parallel and more ornamental expressions of Cooper's own authorial voice, echo the values and the style of Bartram's *Travels*.

Bartram's literary qualities would also interest English Romantic poets such as William Wordsworth and Samuel Taylor Coleridge. Coleridge called Bartram's *Travels* "a work of high merit in every way." He might have drawn on Bartram's colorful nature imagery in some of his own works, including the renowned and imaginative "Rime of the Ancient Mariner."

Bartram also had some illustrious readers whom he knew personally. Although Ben Franklin had died before the *Travels* was published, George Washington and Thomas Jefferson were both intrigued by the book. Jefferson corresponded with Bartram on natural history subjects. Washington wrote approvingly of the *Travels*, and he visited Bartram's Gardens twice during the Constitutional Convention in Philadelphia. The peace of the gardens must have provided welcome escape and refreshment for the stoic leader.

The *Travels* also earned Bartram an international reputation as a natural historian. He corresponded with many colleagues, and he proved to be an intellectually generous mentor to the next generation. The most important of Bartram's proteges was Alexander Wilson, who would become known as the Father of American Ornithology.

Bartram's Paradise

Bartram died in 1823 at eighty-five years of age. His exit came as he was immersed in the work that he loved. He had been sitting at his desk writing an article about the natural history of a plant; then he stood and walked toward the door to take his morning survey of the botanical gardens. On the way, he fell to the floor and did not get up.

William Bartram had lived his life in gardens and nature. It is fitting to close our consideration of him with a look back at one of his favorite places: the Alachua Savanna of central Florida.

It was there that he observed sandhill cranes—he called them savanna cranes—inspiring one of his most endearing sketches. Bartram's crane illustration is full of lively energy and sprightly motion. The crane is prancing along through a peaceful landscape, his elegant wings just slightly outstretched, his head held high. He is full of the natural joy of life.

Bartram portrayed the Alachua Savanna environment with this classic scene of the *Travels*:

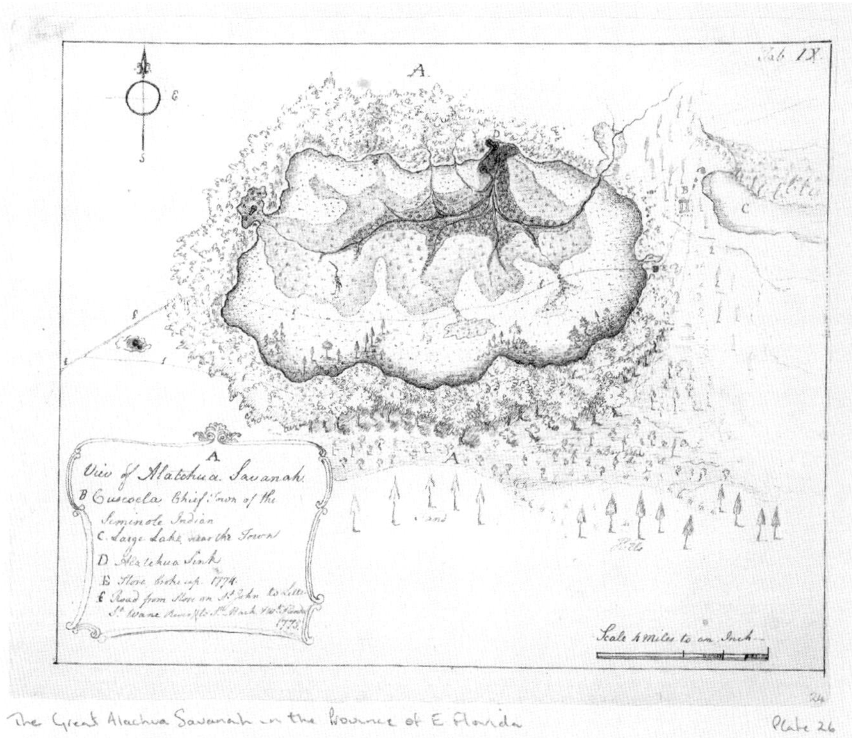

Map of the Alachua Savanna. Today, this beautiful place is preserved as Paynes Prairie State Park. *Courtesy the Roving Naturalists, P.K. Yonge Library of Florida History, Special and Area Studies Collections, George A. Smathers Libraries, University of Florida, Gainesville, Florida.*

> *The glorious sovereign of the day, calling in his bright beaming emanations, left us in his absence to…the silver queen of night, attended by millions of brilliant luminaries. The thundering alligator had ended his horrifying roar; the silver plumed gannet and stork, the sage and solitary pelican of the wilderness, had already retired to their silent nocturnal habitations, in neighboring forests; the sonorous savanna cranes, in well-disciplined squadrons, now rising from the earth, mounted aloft in spiral circles, far from the dense atmosphere of the humid plain; they again viewed the glorious sun, and the light of day still gleaming on their polished feathers, they sung their evening hymn, then in a straight line majestically descended, and alighted on the towering Palms or lofty Pines, their secure and peaceful lodging places.*

Elsewhere, he described cranes as they take flight during the day: "Behold the loud, sonorous, watchful savanna cranes" as "with musical clangour"

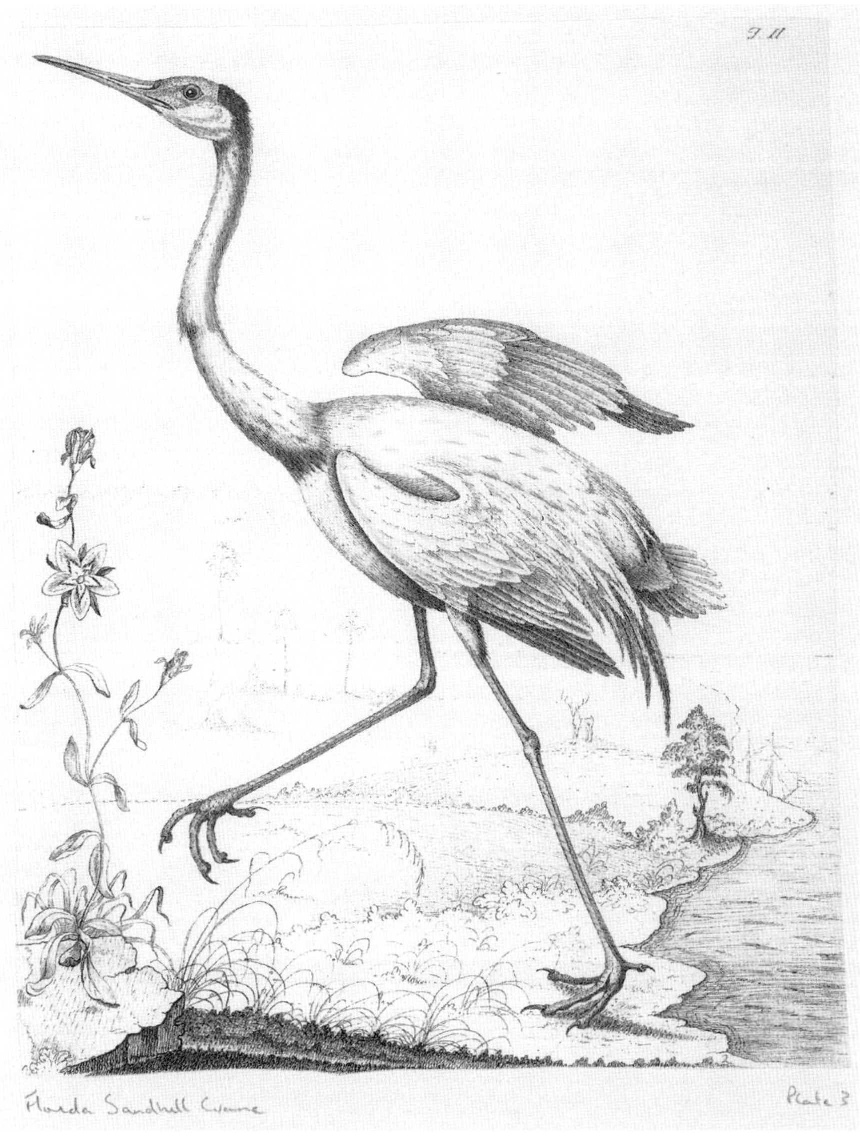

The "savanna crane" was Bartram's name for the sandhill crane, likely because he observed the birds on the Alachua Savanna. This elegant and graceful crane is vibrant with the joy of life. *Courtesy of the Roving Naturalists, P.K. Yonge Library of Florida History, Special and Area Studies Collections, George A. Smathers Libraries, University of Florida, Gainesville, Florida.*

they fly upward, "ascending aloft in spiral circles, bound on interesting discoveries…in the silver regions of the clouded skies." The idea of the cranes as fellow explorers seeking interesting discoveries is a joyous one indeed.

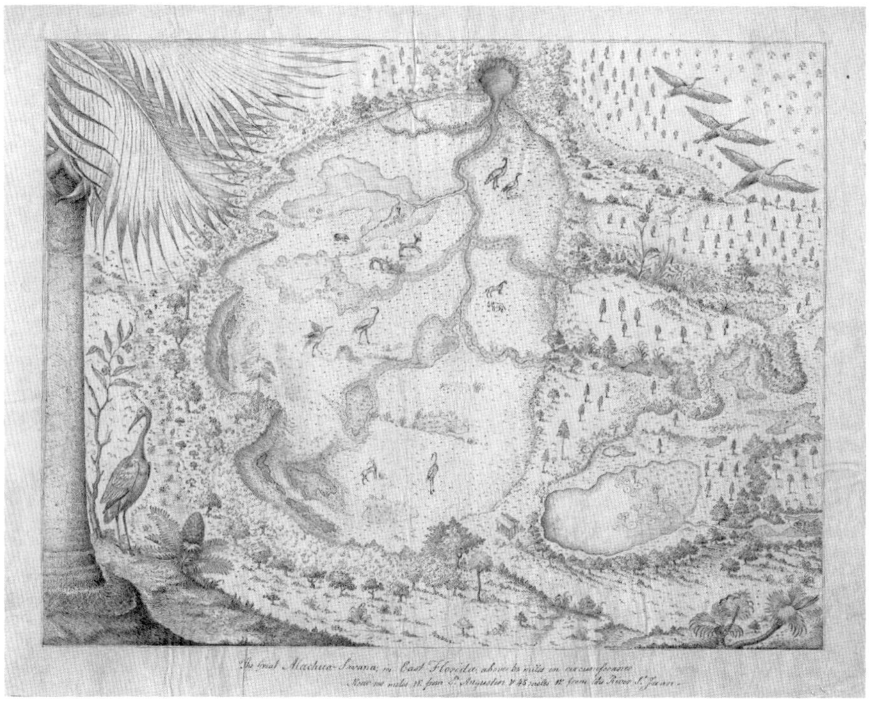

The Alachua Savanna was one of Bartram's favorite places in Florida. This illustrated map features sandhill cranes, deer and horses, as well as a variety of trees. *Courtesy of the American Philosophical Society.*

Such passages of Bartram's writing defy categorization. Are they natural history or poetry? They are both. And they are a call to appreciation. Bartram was a scientist and an artist, and for him the earth was full of wonder. That sense of wonder is what he hoped to inspire through his work.

10

ESCAPE FROM NAPOLEON

Audubon's Origin Story

John James Audubon is the most beloved artist of birds in American history, and with good reason. His skill in close observation, his love for birds and his artistic brilliance all work together harmoniously. Even in our own age of photography, Audubon's images are so detailed and accurate that they can still be used as reference points to identify a species, and at the same time, they are masterpieces of artistry.

Audubon's travels in Florida began amid challenges and difficulties, but his perseverance led to triumphs. Some of his most memorable adventures took place here, leading to classic images in his magnum opus, *Birds of America.* (For the first time in our account, we come to an artist who knew the value of a snappy title.)

The Audubon images that are most familiar are the plates from *Birds of America*. Those plates were based on Audubon's original watercolor paintings. For the production of the book, Audubon worked with a talented British artist and publisher named Robert Havell the Younger. Havell studied the paintings carefully and used them as a basis for the colorful plates that he and his large studio produced. These plates were the images that actually appeared in *Birds of America* and became famous.

When you see an Audubon print hanging on someone's wall today, the odds are that it is a reproduction of one of the plates found in *Birds of America*. However, it is Audubon's original watercolors that are the featured images in the book that you are reading now. Viewing the watercolors allows for some unusual insights into Audubon's work as an artist, as we shall see.

However, to appreciate Audubon's work in Florida, we must begin with his origins. From his escaping conscription in Napoleon's war machine to his historic experiments with bird banding, Audubon's life experiences gave him an eclectic and adventurous perspective that served him well in the varied environments he would traverse in Florida.

A Case of Identity

Consider this unusual description of St. Augustine, which Audubon gave in a letter to his wife: "St. Augustine resembles some old French village." Old, yes—St. Augustine was already old. And since it was still a city on the edge of a frontier, it did resemble a village. But why *French*? In view of the colonial history of St. Augustine, would not an "old Spanish village" have been a more natural comparison?

The answer is that, although St. Augustine was not particularly French, Audubon was. He was comparing the venerable Floridian city to an old European village, and his frame of reference for European villages was French. John James was once Jean Jacques. When he would later portray himself as the "American Woodsman" and dress in buckskins while attending fashionable events in London, he was playing a role and doing so with the enthusiasm of a foreigner. By way of analogy, there is a scene in John Ford's classic film *The Quiet Man* where John Wayne's character, an Irish American who has moved to Ireland, is painting the door of his cottage a bright green. One of his neighbors sees the color and comments: "Only an American would think of Kelly green!" The John Wayne character was an outsider plunging enthusiastically into what he perceived to be local traditions. Likewise, for someone with Audubon's French background and education, the American Woodsman was an exotic role, and it was one to which he brought considerable flair. Perhaps only a Frenchman would have thought of buckskins.

Audubon also knew that the role was good marketing. His real background was every bit as interesting a story—it just didn't lend itself as naturally to promoting a book about American bird life. Besides, he himself likely had some questions about his family history—and some secrets that he did not want to share with the world.

Audubon was born in 1785 in the Caribbean, on the island then known as Saint Domingue or Santo Domingo (today Haiti). His father was a French captain and owner of a plantation on Santo Domingo; his mother was a maidservant. They were not married, and the infant Jean Jacques Rabin (he was known then by his mother's family name) seems to have been one of multiple illegitimate children that his father had with multiple women. By the standards of any century, Captain Audubon was far from an upstanding character.

John James Audubon was living at a time when illegitimate birth carried a very real social stigma. In the autobiographical account that he would write for his own children, he sought to lend both respectability and romance to the story of his parents. He claimed that his father had "married a lady of Spanish extraction, whom I have been led to understand was as beautiful as she was wealthy" and who became his mother. Audubon was likely trying to save himself embarrassment and maintain family privacy (and family secrets). The words "I have been led to understand" are interesting, as they suggest that he was relating what was told to him in childhood; they might imply his own doubts and questions. A surviving letter from his father provides evidence that Audubon was eventually told the truth about his birth—a truth that he then chose not to share.

Despite the deception, there is something touching about the desire of John James Audubon to romanticize the story of his parents. He knew there was more to life than brief liaisons; he himself had a long and happy marriage, and he observed loyal unions even among some species of birds. He might have had numerous motives, both social and very personal, in trying to rewrite his own family history.

Birds of France

Audubon's mother died at a very young age, and his father "adopted" him and brought him to France. By this time, his father had married a wealthy French woman. Audubon was raised in their home in Nantes, on the Loire River, and in their country home in the village of Coueron.

Audubon loved exploring the French countryside. Soon, he was assembling a collection of natural curiosities, including birds' nests and eggs, as well as flowers and lichens. The only problem was that these early natural history expeditions often took place while he was supposed to be in school. His father commended his collection while also trying to steer him toward an interest in formal education—with limited success.

The love of nature, the special interest in birds and the artistic inclination, all of which would be so central to Audubon's life, were part of who he was even from these early days. He later wrote, "During all these years there existed within me a tendency to follow Nature in her walks. Perhaps not an hour of leisure was spent elsewhere than in the woods and the fields, and to examine either the eggs, nest, young, or parents of any species of birds constituted my delight. It was about this period that I commenced a series of drawings of the birds of France, which I continued until I had upwards of two hundred drawings." Thus, *Birds of America* was long preceded by a prospective *Birds of France*.

However, Audubon would eventually take the nearly universal view of artists considering their own early work—the drawings were "all bad enough," he said. Interestingly, though, he added this remark: "Yet they were representations of birds." The skills needed development, but the love was already there.

REVOLUTION AND EMPIRE

Audubon's artistic skills would need a different field in order to flourish, however. The revolution was sweeping over France. Soon there was a guillotine in the city plaza of Nantes. With their wealth, the Audubons themselves were in danger, although their naval connections might have provided some degree of protection. This was one period of his life that John James Audubon would refuse to write about. After alluding to it in the autobiographical essay for his children, he said, "Let me forever drop the curtain over the frightful aspect of this dire picture. To think of those dreadful days is too terrible." Here and here alone, the great storyteller was silent.

Eventually, the internal violence of the French Revolution was redirected outward, with the rise of Napoleon Bonaparte and his grandiose imperialism. This opened a new danger for young Audubon, who was now at precisely the age when he would be a target for conscription. What a loss it would have been, for art and for natural history, had Audubon been pressed into the French military and died on a field of battle or in the cannon fire of a naval engagement.

Thankfully, his father arranged his escape. By this point, Captain Audubon had no desire to see his son follow him into the navy; on the contrary, he wanted his boy to be as far as possible from the military machine of Bonaparte's France. Thus, he obtained a false passport for his son and sent him off to America under an alias. In cloak-and-dagger style, young Audubon escaped by sea and sailed to the New World.

Perhaps from the rigors of the voyage, he suffered a bout of yellow fever soon after his arrival. When he regained his health, he would settle—at least temporarily—on a Pennsylvania farm that his father had purchased as an investment. Known as Mill Grove, the farm would be the site of some important developments in Audubon's young life.

Soon, the eighteen-year-old John James Audubon (he had now anglicized his name) was exploring the countryside of Pennsylvania as eagerly as he had explored the fields and forests of France. The environments were very different, but his love of nature was the same. And he would always be grateful for the peace, as well as the opportunities for discovery, that life in America afforded him. Although he would face considerable financial struggles, Audubon was able to sketch in peace while the Napoleonic Wars from which he had escaped ran their course. By 1821, when Bonaparte died in exile on St. Helena, Audubon had begun his work on *Birds of America*.

There is a curious afterword to this saga. Napoleon Bonaparte had a nephew, Charles Lucien, who became an ornithologist. Audubon eventually met Charles Lucien Bonaparte, and a lengthy and complex correspondence ensued. Sometimes, they were friendly and professionally supportive of each other, while at other times, a rivalry emerged, and they could be quite acerbic. In one letter, Audubon referred to "your great-uncle Napoleon to whom I have reason to feel greatly indebted." Was he being serious or sarcastic? Paradoxically, perhaps both. His flight from Napoleonic conscription had led him to North America, where he met his beloved wife and found a new frontier for his studies of birds. So maybe the words were earnest, grateful and sardonic all at the same time.

The Silver Thread

Audubon would never forget the day when he visited a nearby farm to introduce himself to his neighbors. The man of the house was not at home, but he was welcomed into the parlor to await his return. The farmer's daughter was a beautiful young lady with a kindly manner. Her name was Lucy Bakewell, and young Audubon soon fell in love with her. In time, she would become his wife.

It was also at Mill Grove that Audubon made a historic experiment with bird banding. The idea of banding had originated with falconry centuries before. Its value to natural history studies is suggested by a story from the sixteenth century. A peregrine falcon prized by King Henry IV of France escaped; the falcon was found in Malta—after a swift journey—and recognized by its band. By the late seventeenth and early eighteenth centuries, the banding of gray herons in Europe and Asia Minor was providing information about longevity and migration patterns. In the rustic environment of his Mill Grove farm, Audubon pioneered the use of banding in North America, using it to learn about the migration of birds on this continent.

It was not only Audubon's love of birds but also his curiosity about them that led to the ingenious project. Picture the sights and sounds of a northern spring—the song of birds heard once again as migrants arrive in familiar fields and forests. Audubon welcomed their return, but he wondered, were they really the same individuals returning? It is one thing to identify a species but how to determine whether they were the same individual birds?

He had an answer in mind. He had been observing a nest of eastern phoebes, and he noticed that the birds were becoming habituated to his presence and comfortable around him. He therefore experimented by tying a silver thread around the leg of each young one. The following spring, he found that some of the eastern phoebes who had returned to nest in the area had silver threads on their legs. The experiment had proven that these migratory birds were returning to their old homes.

Today, some writers claim that Audubon exaggerated the results or even that he made up the story, noting, for example, that he had temporarily returned to France during the time period that he references. It is true that he journeyed to France at around this time—a chivalrous quest to ask his father's blessing on his wish to marry Lucy. However, Audubon acknowledges the trip to France in his account of the banding and simply states that he continued his observations when he returned. In any case, Audubon's account became famous, and it certainly promoted the use of banding in the study of bird migration. Today, banding is widely recognized as an important method in ornithology.

THE AMERICAN WOODSMAN

In time, John James Audubon became something of a migratory creature himself. After he married Lucy, they moved to Kentucky to open a trading post. The business failed, and a long period of financial struggle ensued. Nevertheless, the couple remained devoted to each other. Audubon later wrote of his wife: "Her brave and cheerful spirit accepted all, and no reproaches from her beloved lips ever wounded my heart. With her was I not always rich?"

Along with such reassurances of sincere love, the hardships of this period had another silver lining, since they led Audubon into work that would be far more useful to his art than selling provisions at a frontier trading post. He began painting portraits to earn money; he also did taxidermy work for a natural history museum in Cincinnati. Those two pursuits would be curiously united in the artwork that would become his legacy.

Another factor was his 1810 meeting with Alexander Wilson, a protege of William Bartram. Wilson's illustrated book, *American Ornithology*, provided inspiration in both a positive and negative sense. It was scientifically important, and it featured colorful illustrations of North American birds. However, due to budgetary considerations, Wilson tried to cram as many species as possible onto each color plate. Thus, while his images were accurate from the standpoint of ornithology, their artistic appeal was limited. They seemed busy and random, and background landscapes were sparse or nonexistent. Audubon realized that the science of North American ornithology could be explored in a far more artistic way.

Eventually, he conceived the ambitious idea of publishing a beautifully illustrated book that would cover as many North American bird species as possible. There was just one problem: the family was struggling to make a living. Lucy's relatives thought Audubon was out of his mind. Nevertheless, he put together some money he had made from portraiture and other work and gave it to Lucy to provide for her and his children while he was gone. He also arranged for them to live for a while with his brother-in-law, who was far more successful financially. Then, Audubon set forth on his quixotic journey. He would spend years trekking through forests and traveling on the Mississippi, seeking out birds to study and sketch.

Louisiana became an important field of operations, and in time, he sent for Lucy and the children to join him there. Meanwhile, like so many artists before him, he sought patronage. In 1824, some of his work was displayed in Philadelphia at the Academy of Natural Sciences, but the exhibit failed to garner him support. Alexander Wilson had become a kind of adoptive favorite son in Philadelphia, and Audubon was his rival.

Eventually, Audubon decided that his New World project could best be supported with Old World patronage. After earning some money through a stint as a fencing teacher—a legacy of his privileged upbringing in France—he set sail for Great Britain. The year was 1826.

When Audubon stepped off the ship and onto English soil, he might have felt like a new man. He certainly acted like one. Audubon had developed a new persona for himself, highly fictionalized but based on his real-life experiences. By now, he had run a frontier trading post (albeit unsuccessfully) and had spent considerable time traveling through the North American wilderness studying birds. These adventures, along with his flair for the theatrical, led to his self-characterization as the "American Woodsman," which he debuted in England to great effect.

The frontier adventure novels of James Fenimore Cooper—so greatly influenced by William Bartram—were by now beloved in England. And here was John James Audubon dressing in buckskins and acting like a character straight from the pages of *The Last of the Mohicans*. In rented halls and at fashionable dinner parties, he showed his watercolors of birds. The background of the paintings showed the birds' natural habitats—distinctive North American landscapes. Audubon also did mimicry, imitating the hoots of owls and the purported battle cries of Native American tribes. (The owl sounds, at least, were accurate.) It was a spectacular use of blarney (or the French equivalent), backed up by the genuine artistic talent reflected in the watercolors. Soon, Audubon had valuable contacts in both London and Edinburgh, and the complex process of producing and publishing *Birds of America* was underway.

The book was issued in multiple volumes during the following years. In 1829, Audubon returned to America for an emotional reunion with Lucy. The year after that, he and Lucy sailed for England together. Like Catesby before him, Audubon was honored with a Fellowship in the Royal Society. But crossing the Atlantic was becoming a familiar theme in his life. He and his wife returned to America, and he returned to his field work; further observations, specimens and paintings were needed for the upcoming volumes of *Birds of America*. One of his destinations would be Florida.

Since William Bartram's time, Florida had undergone two changes of flags. The British had handed it back to the Spanish at the end of the American Revolution. This Spanish period ended in 1821, when Florida became a territory of the United States.

Audubon would make important trips to Florida during 1831 and 1832. The expeditions in Florida are the focus of our look at John James Audubon. The wilds of the St. John's River country presented him with unexpected challenges. Yet he would eventually find himself enchanted by the amazing bird life of the marshes, coasts and islands, and his Floridian expeditions would be crowned with grand success.

11

PELICANS, A FAITHFUL DOG AND SWASHBUCKLING CARACARAS

St. Augustine and the St. John's River

Audubon's early adventures in Florida would bring him through territory that his predecessor Bartram had also covered. He began by using St. Augustine as a kind of base camp, and it is during this time that he wrote about how the city reminded him of a French provincial village. He found lodgings in a tavern where the menu met with his approval. (It included venison and fresh fish.) From St. Augustine, he set forth on a river voyage, exploring the St. John's and the surrounding shores.

However, as a nineteenth-century traveler—half a century on from William Bartram—and as a man whose work was already drawing attention on both sides of the Atlantic, John James Audubon was not traveling by dugout canoe. He was a passenger on a U.S. Navy schooner, the *Spark*.

On coming aboard and being welcomed by the lieutenant in command, Audubon was quickly impressed by the naval order that prevailed aboard the vessel. "The strict attention to duty on board even this small vessel of war afforded a matter of surprise to me," he later wrote. "Everything went on with the regularity of a chronometer: orders were given, answered to and accomplished before they ceased to vibrate on the ear. The neatness of the crew equaled the cleanliness of the white planks of the deck; the sails were in perfect condition; and, built as the *Spark* was, for swift sailing, on she went gamboling from wave to wave." It all seemed to point to a pleasant and prosperous voyage ahead. At least for the first few minutes.

No sooner had the *Spark* reached the mouth of the river than a storm arose. Dark clouds filled the sky, the winds were contrary and the whole expedition was postponed, with the schooner anchoring in the protection of St. Augustine's harbor.

In time, the storm passed, and the voyage began again. A navigational hazard was soon encountered, but the commander was prepared for it. There were sandbars that had to be crossed at high tide with the assistance of a local pilot. Time and tide were with the *Spark*, and a gun was fired to signal the pilot that his services were needed. At first, there was no response, and Audubon suspected that they were interrupting a nap, but the firing of a second gun led to the appearance of a canoe beside the schooner; the pilot had arrived after all. With his knowledge, and with the favorable tide, the *Spark* made it—just barely—across the sandbar.

Audubon's attention was already elsewhere, though. An enormous flock of white pelicans had appeared.

The Nobility of Pelicans

"My eyes," he recalled, "were not directed towards the waters but on high, where flew some thousands of snowy Pelicans which had fled affrighted from their nesting grounds." The signal guns had startled them into action. Audubon watched in wonder. "How beautifully they performed their broad gyrations, and how matchless after awhile was the marshaling of their files as they flew past us!"

Such admiration for pelicans would also be expressed in Audubon's portraits of them. Consider his profile view of the American white pelican. The bird has a stalwart stance. There is an air of nobility that is enhanced, rather than lessened, by its ungainly appearance. This is a portrait of character. Audubon might have been inspired by the history of the pelican in literature and art—from its use as a symbol of loneliness and dejection in the biblical psalms to its role as an emblem of chivalry and honor on mediaeval heraldic crests. Without sacrificing scientific accuracy, he managed to endow the pelican with the manner of an unlikely knight. If that seems like a contradiction, just spend some time watching pelicans in real life.

A bold compositional choice also marks this image. Most of Audubon's birds, as we will see, were placed in the composition that includes a landscape backdrop. The white pelican does have such a backdrop—a maritime scene—but in this case, the bird is taking up almost the entire space. His tail feathers nearly brush the edge of the frame, so to speak, while on the other side, the tiny curve at the tip of his enormous bill also comes close to the edge. His head, bold and bright against a clouded sky, is near the top border, and his webbed feet, poised on a rocky shore, are near the bottom. The effect is to emphasize the bird's large size, as well as the air of valor that the whole portrait seems to convey.

There is likewise a sense of dignity in Audubon's brown pelican. Here, too, Audubon portrayed the bird in profile, with a single bright eye gazing out at the viewer. As we will see, Audubon was highly skilled at portraying birds in motion. Thus, he was making a deliberate choice in showing both the white and brown pelicans as still and calm. Instead of highlighting energy and action, as he sometimes would, he established a sense of gravitas.

Audubon portrayed the brown pelican on a branch. Its webbed feet are shown in detail, but they are slightly curled, as if the pelican is attempting to perch without really being a perching bird. It is possible that Audubon wanted to give a physical tension to the feet to show the resulting creases and wrinkles, which he does in great detail. This is analogous to a classical sculptor portraying a figure in an athletic pose to use the technique of spiral torsion, thereby showing the strain of the muscles. Audubon, though, is using such tension only in the feet; the rest of the brown pelican's body is calm. This makes for an interesting contrast and highlights the exceedingly fine detail of Audubon's art.

Considering that the profile views of the white pelican and the brown pelican are similar in concept, there are interesting contrasts between them. The feet of the white pelican are flat on the rocky shore. The brown pelican is poised on a branch with leaves and seed pods, but it is set against a bare backdrop. The white pelican stands against a sky full of gray clouds, with blue gray waves lapping the stony shoreline near its feet. The two birds are facing in opposite directions. Even without the differences in plumage color, the portraits of these two pelicans would in no way be redundant.

This shows the great variety that Audubon brought to his compositions. It is a trait that makes his art accessible and appealing even to audiences uninterested in purely scientific studies of birds. It is also a trait that brings us back to the first artist whose work we considered—Mark Catesby. In his time, Catesby was a pioneer in bringing scientific images of birds and animals together with elements of landscape painting. His connections were sometimes random, as in the strange case of the flamingo and the coral, but he was interested in providing colorful backdrops. That idea would be continued, and brought to a far higher level, with the artistry of Audubon. A key feature of Audubon's work was his ability to place his painted birds in realistic painted habitats—habitats that were both beautiful and natural.

A Newfoundland in Florida

The majestic sight of thousands of white pelicans must have seemed an auspicious beginning to the voyage. However, the trip would soon become quite uncomfortable, as Audubon was exposed to an aspect of the natural world that did not excite his admiration: Florida's abundant insects. "The 'blind mosquitoes' covered every object even in the cabin," he complained. Individually tiny but appearing in an aggravating swarm, they would probably be called no-see-ums today. Audubon was trying to update his journal by candlelight, but the insects were so numerous in the cabin that clouds of them virtually extinguished the flickering candle flame. When Audubon closed the book in frustration, "more than a hundred of the little wretches" were crushed between the leaves of his pages.

Along with such irritations, Audubon was disappointed by a lack of sightings during the rest of his voyage aboard the *Spark*. The spectacle of the white pelicans was followed by a dry spell, save for a few wading birds that could be seen at most Floridian bodies of water. In a letter afterward, Audubon would describe his expedition aboard the *Spark* as "a complete failure," an expression perhaps prompted by fatigue as well as disappointment. (During the same period, he also grumbled about how wading through the salt marshes ruined his socks—a complaint not exactly in keeping with his self-invented character as the American Woodsman.)

In any case, Audubon left the *Spark* and found a boat of his own in which to return to St. Augustine. This, too, would prove to be a misadventure. However, this is an appropriate juncture at which to introduce another character in the story. Audubon was not traveling alone; his faithful dog was with him.

The dog was a Newfoundland named Plato. The breed might seem out of place in Florida, but Newfoundlands are good retrievers, a trait that was valuable to Audubon. However, he did worry about Plato in Florida, not so much because of the heat but because of the alligators. Newfoundlands love water, but Audubon wisely made sure to keep Plato out of the rivers and lakes.

Audubon's love of dogs is reflected, along with many other aspects of his character, in a notable portrait. The portrait was actually painted by one of his children—a son named John Woodhouse Audubon who followed in his father's artistic footsteps. The painting shows John James on one of his expeditions, with a landscape of forests and fields behind him and a sky tinged with the colors of dawn or sunset. He is seated on a rock or a low hill, with a long rifle in his hand for the procurement of specimens; he is dressed in a coat, a gray suit and a white shirt with a high, unbuttoned collar. His hair ranges in color from iron gray to dove gray and flows past his shoulders; he is clean-shaven, but his sideburns are very long (and nearly white). His face is tilted to the side, and his bright eyes gaze past the viewer and into the distance—doubtless scanning the horizon for interesting birds. The portrait is affectionate and rich in characterization. And on the ground next to Audubon, curled up contentedly at his side, is a furry brown and white dog. The dog might be a Newfoundland; though today they are usually thought of as having solidly black fur, black and white or brown and white were familiar variations for the breed in the nineteenth century. In any case, the portrait certainly attests to Audubon's habit of bringing a faithful dog with him on his expeditions.

During the journey back to St. Augustine, Plato would end up being a kind of guide dog. The last part of the trip was on foot. Audubon and the two locals he had hired to accompany him planned to procure a wagon, but there were no wagons to be had, so they instead found themselves hiking through a pine barren while the sun was setting and the weather growing ominous. "The air felt hot and oppressive, and we knew that a tempest was approaching." They pressed on boldly, led by Plato. "Plato was now our guide, the white spots on his coat being the only objects that we could discern." He seemed to know that he was leading his master, because he continued to stay slightly ahead on the trail.

Soon, the travelers had to press on through the storm. "Vivid flashes of lightning streamed across the heavens, the wind increased to a gale and the rain poured down upon us like a torrent…but at length the tempest passed over and suddenly the clear sky became spangled with stars." Their relief became even greater when they realized that they were nearing their destination. "We smelt the salt marshes and walking directly toward them like pointers advancing upon a covey of partridges we at last to our great joy described the light of the beacon near St. Augustine." Plato was as excited as his master. "My dog began to run briskly around, having met with ground on which he had hunted before, and taking a direct course led us to the great causeway that crosses the marshes at the back of the town." Audubon and Plato were soon safely back at the tavern.

AVIAN ENERGY AND ARTISTIC INGENUITY

An important observation in the St. Augustine area came not during the misadventure of the *Spark* but while Audubon was on horseback exploring the lands surrounding the city. There, he spotted a caracara. Not only was this an interesting discovery for him, but it also furnished a dramatic scene in *Birds of America*. Audubon would portray the caracara with energy and motion, contrasting markedly with his calm, steady pelicans.

The caracara was a discovery for Audubon because although he had read of it as a South American bird, he had not known that it was found in the United States. To be sure, Florida is one of the northern edges of this remarkable creature's distribution. The caracara has the appearance of a bird of prey, perhaps a small eagle or a large hawk; however, like the vulture, it is a carrion feeder. Its most unforgettable feature is its pale blue beak. Audubon's image shows two caracaras, and the shade of blue that he used for their beaks is perfectly chosen; it is vibrant yet pale, like a cheerful pastel, and very true to life. He even conveyed the subtle reflection of light on the surfaces of the beaks.

The two caracaras in the image are in combat, and the work of art is a great example of the theatrical flair that was an important part of Audubon's repertoire. One caracara is in flight, plunging downward toward the other. The second caracara is perched on a branch, its body bent and face upturned as it tries to deflect its attacker. This work of art is very much a scene of action and portrays the caracaras in a swashbuckling aerial duel.

The ability to convey an illusion of motion was, in fact, one of the keys to Audubon's success as an artist. To achieve this, he used an ingenious technique. Like many inventions, it began as an attempt to solve a problem.

Place yourself in the artist's shoes. You want to paint wild birds with realism and vitality. Clearly, the best way to do so is to paint them from life. However, the birds are not going to helpfully pose for you. To really understand Audubon's difficulty, think about wildlife photography today—the challenge of finding the right moment to get the perfect photo—and now imagine replacing your camera with a sketchpad and a palette. Now add to this another challenge: you have set the goal of painting not only certain selected birds but as many North American species as possible.

Audubon therefore made the decision to work from specimens. The American Woodsman was a skilled hunter, and he had worked with taxidermy for a museum of natural history. Thus, he would shoot birds and preserve them as specimens in order to paint them. This may seem

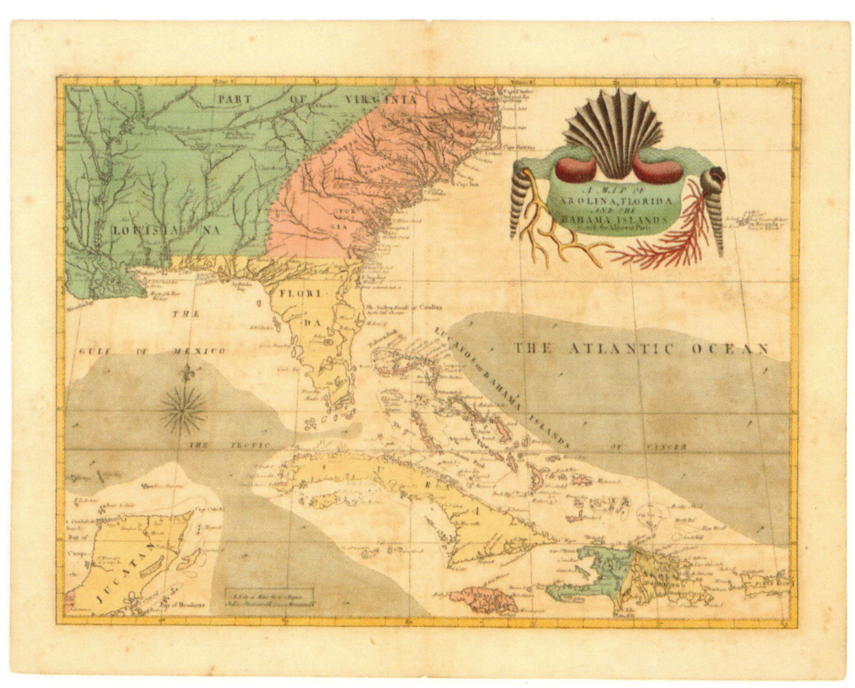

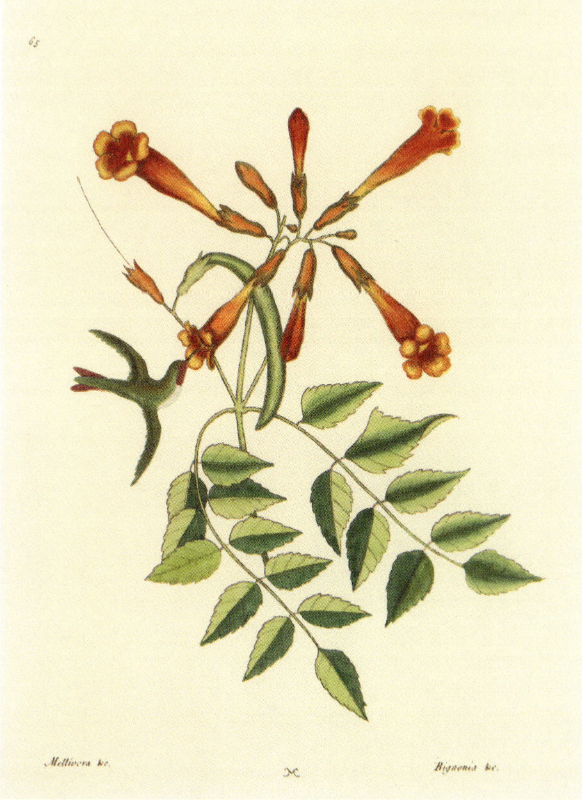

Above: The map that Catesby included with his book is a colorful image, and its legend evokes a heraldic crest. *Mark Catesby, courtesy of the Wilson Library, University of North Carolina, Chapel Hill.*

Left: Catesby's illustration of the ruby-throated hummingbird, which he knew simply as *the* hummingbird, feeding on nectar from the flowers of the trumpet-creeper. *Mark Catesby, courtesy of the Wilson Library, University of North Carolina, Chapel Hill.*

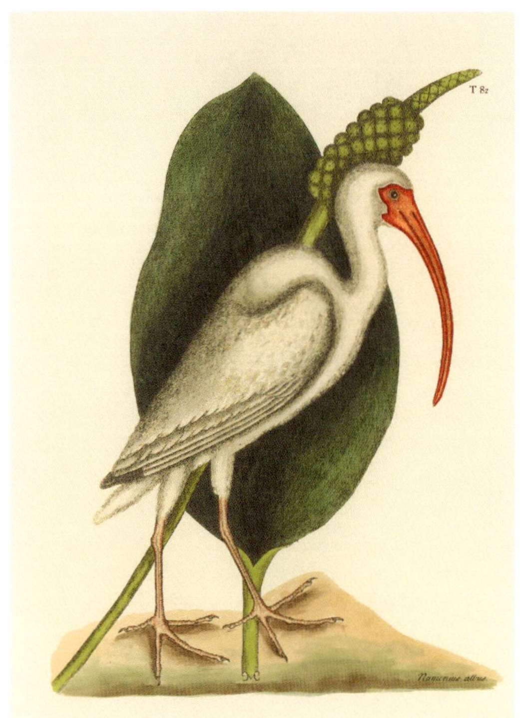

Catesby's lack of concern with scale is seen in his image of the white ibis, which he knew as the white curlew, paired with the golden club plant. *Mark Catesby, courtesy of the Wilson Library, University of North Carolina, Chapel Hill.*

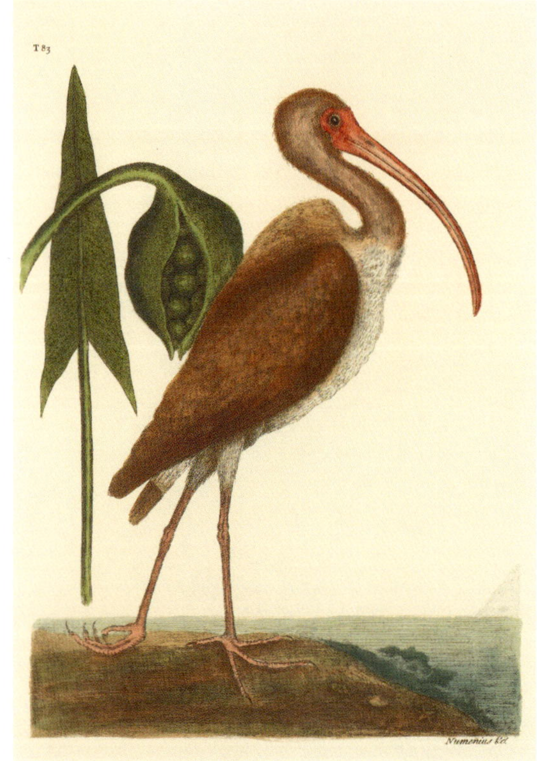

Tricked by the differences in coloring, Catesby thought the juvenile white ibis was a separate species and called it the brown curlew. *Mark Catesby, courtesy of the Wilson Library, University of North Carolina, Chapel Hill.*

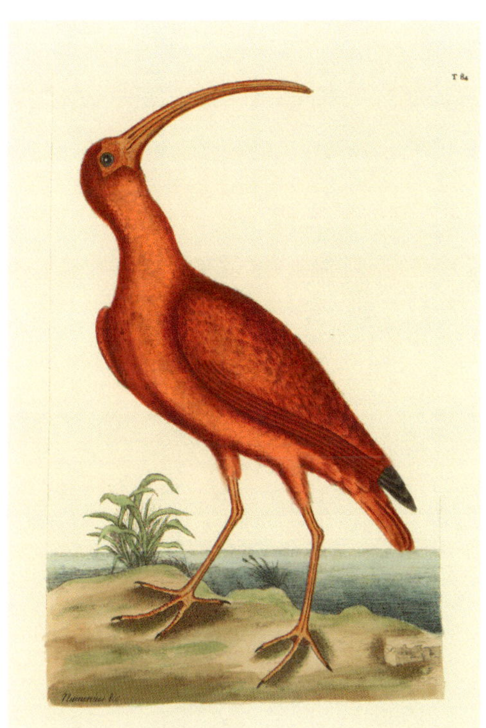

The flamboyant scarlet ibis is a bird Catesby might have seen while he was in the Bahamas. He called it the red curlew. *Mark Catesby, courtesy of the Wilson Library, University of North Carolina, Chapel Hill.*

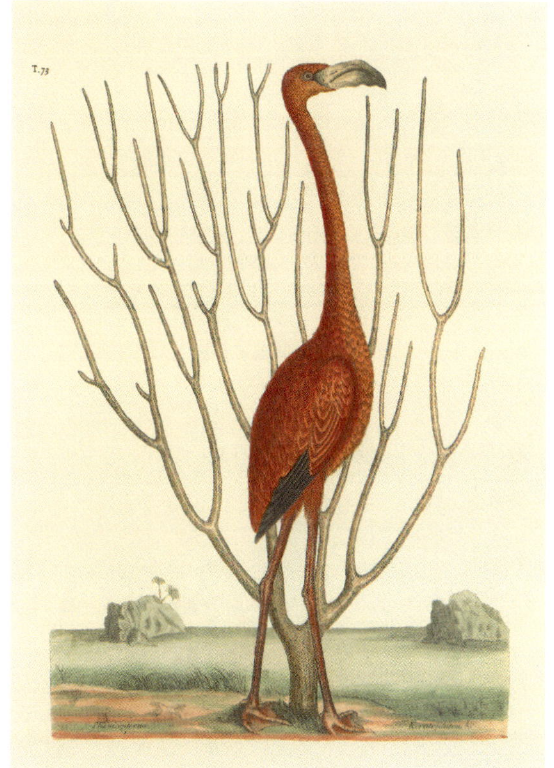

Catesby's picture of the flamingo is surprising and unforgettable. *Mark Catesby, courtesy of the Wilson Library, University of North Carolina, Chapel Hill.*

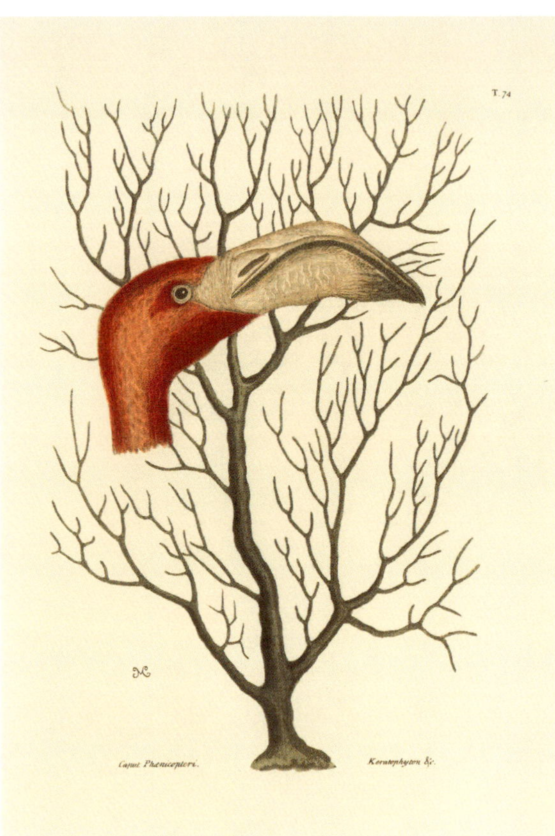

Left: Here, Catesby provided a close-up view of the flamingo's head and bill. Again, the flamingo is mysteriously paired with a piece of coral. *Mark Catesby, courtesy of the Wilson Library, University of North Carolina, Chapel Hill.*

Below: The rice bird, today known as the bobolink, was a key species in a historic paper about migration that Catesby presented to the Royal Society. *Mark Catesby, courtesy of the Wilson Library, University of North Carolina, Chapel Hill.*

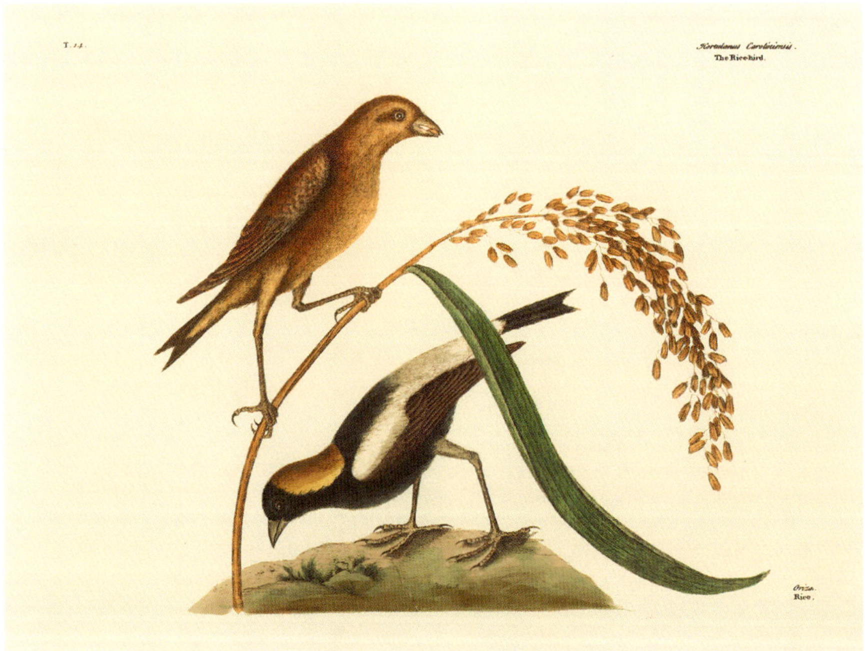

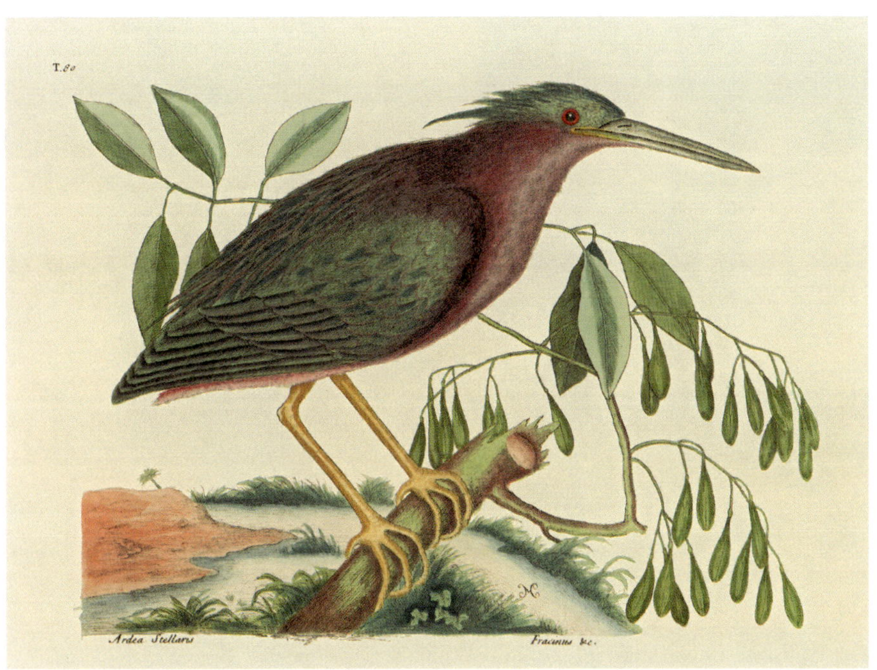

Catesby's green heron—he called it the small bittern—can be compared and contrasted with the green heron portrayals by William Bartram and John James Audubon. *Mark Catesby, courtesy of the Wilson Library, University of North Carolina, Chapel Hill.*

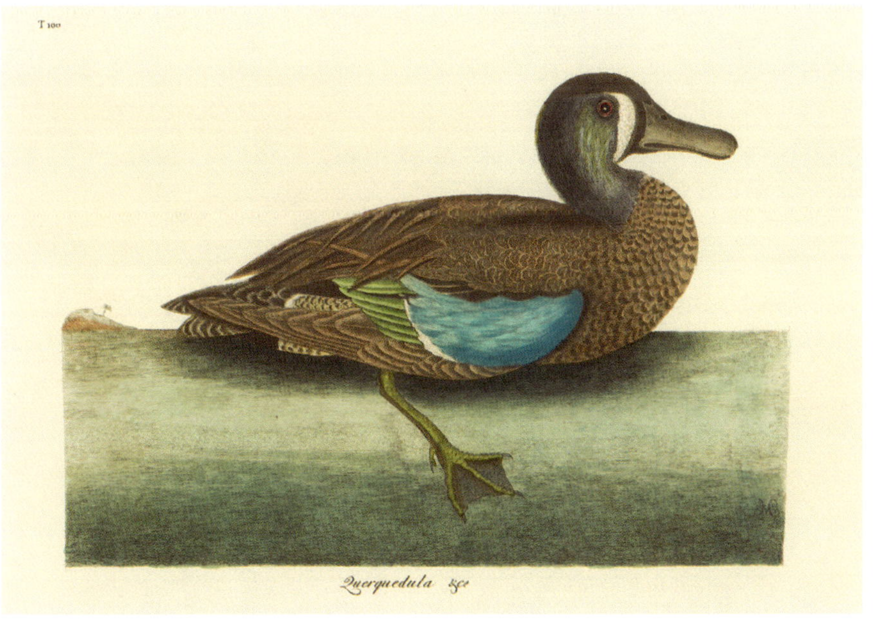

The blue-winged teal, which Catesby called the white-faced teal, further shows the range of Catesby's bird illustrations. *Mark Catesby, courtesy of the Wilson Library, University of North Carolina, Chapel Hill.*

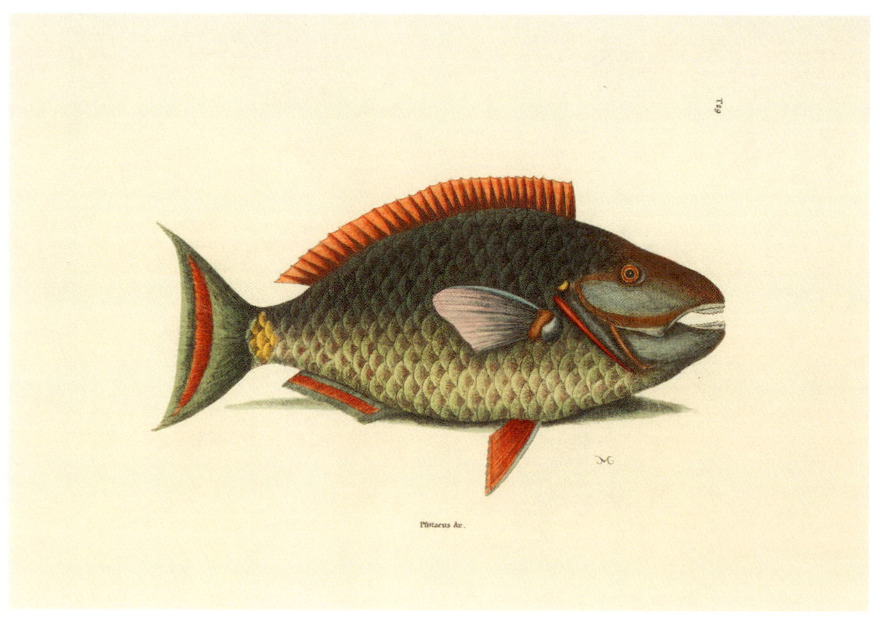

Catesby's book also included illustrations of fish; this parrotfish is a colorful example. *Mark Catesby, courtesy of the Wilson Library, University of North Carolina, Chapel Hill.*

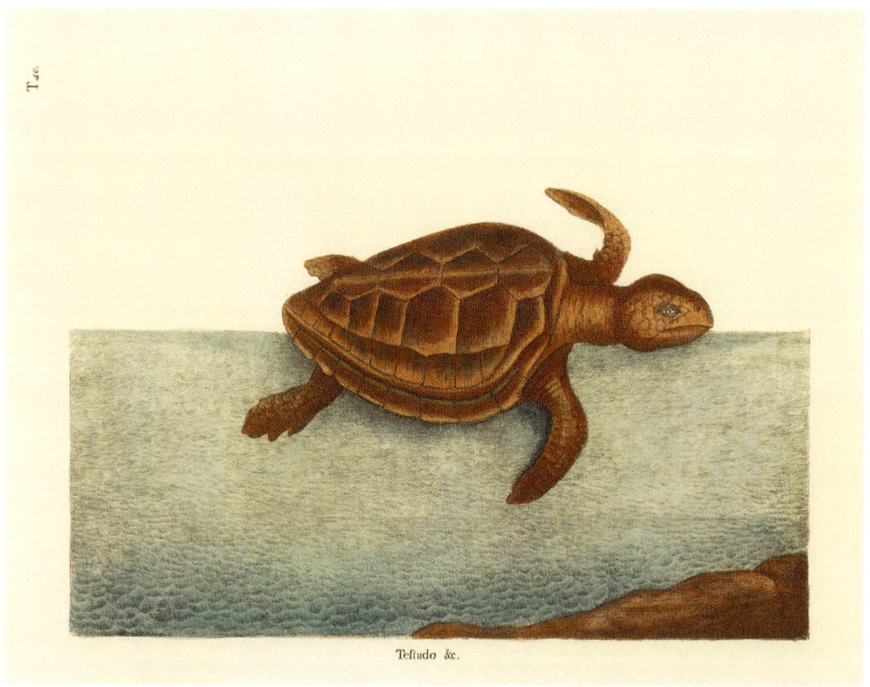

This loggerhead sea turtle is one of three sea turtle species that Catesby illustrated. (The others were the green and the hawksbill.) *Mark Catesby, courtesy of the Wilson Library, University of North Carolina, Chapel Hill.*

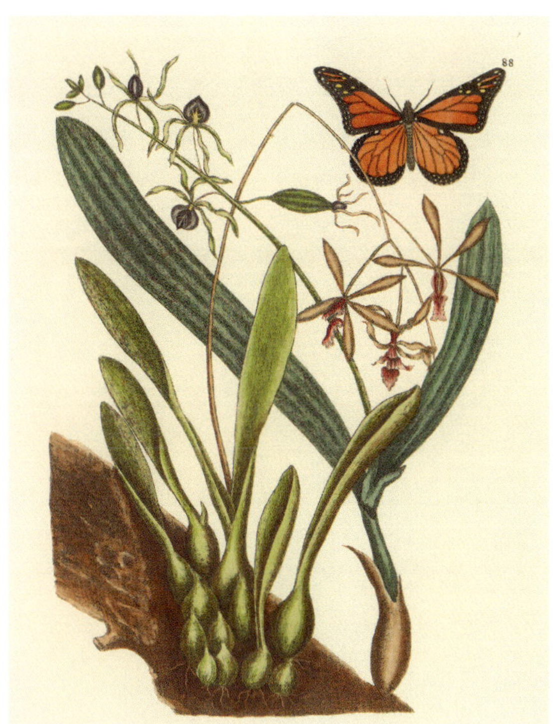

Catesby identified this New World butterfly only with an incomplete Latin name, but it is recognizably the monarch. *Mark Catesby, courtesy of the Wilson Library, University of North Carolina, Chapel Hill.*

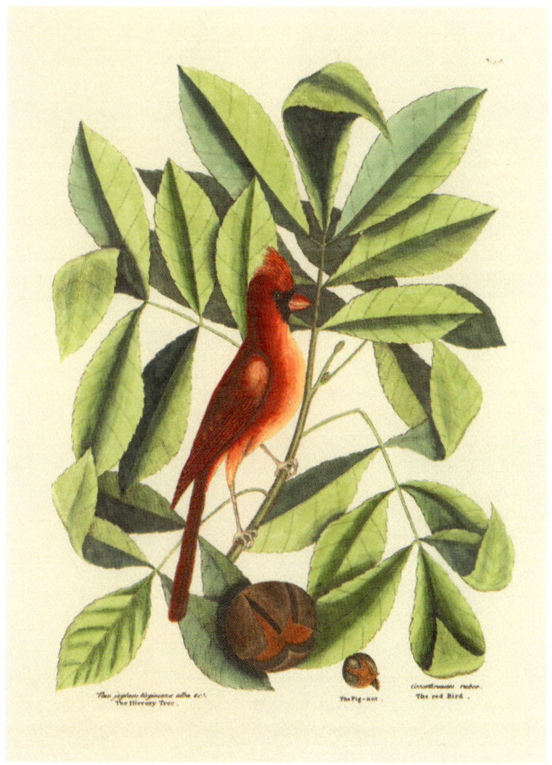

Catesby's "red bird," the northern cardinal, seems to have a whimsical expression. *Mark Catesby, courtesy of the Wilson Library, University of North Carolina, Chapel Hill.*

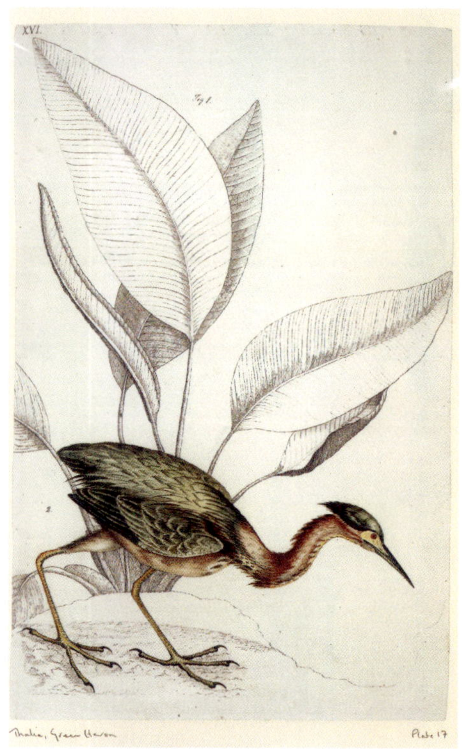

Like Mark Catesby and John James Audubon, Bartram portrayed the green heron. *William Bartram, courtesy of the Roving Naturalists, P.K. Yonge Library of Florida History, Special and Area Studies Collections, George A. Smathers Libraries, University of Florida, Gainesville, Florida.*

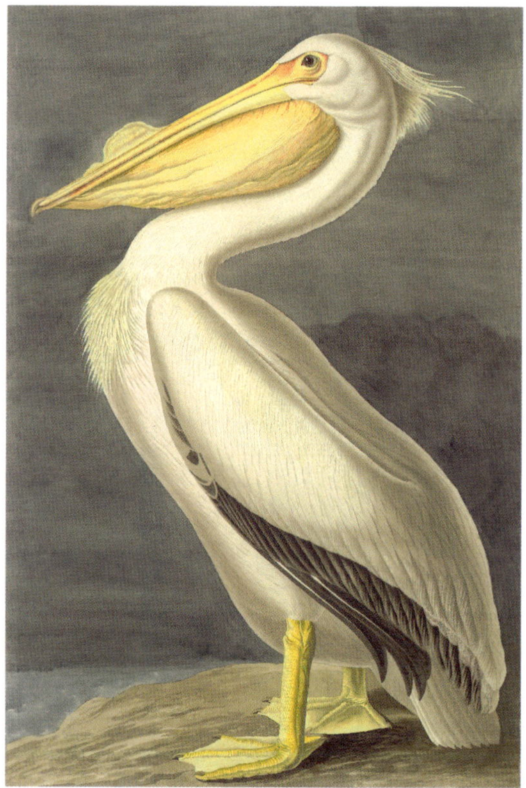

The American white pelican. Audubon saw thousands of these birds while voyaging on the St. John's River. *John James Audubon, digital image created by Oppenheimer Editions. Collection of the New-York Historical Society.*

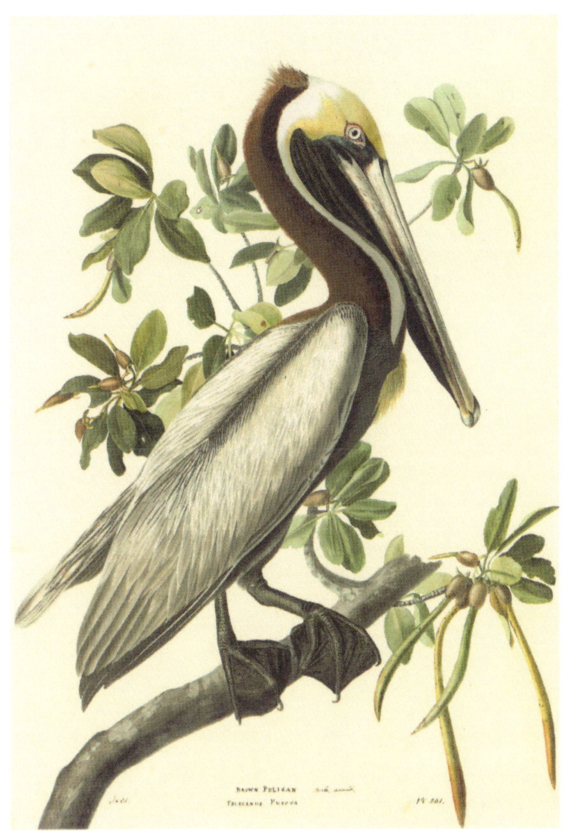

The brown pelican. Audubon portrayed pelicans with great dignity and nobility. *Digital image created by Oppenheimer Editions. Collection of the New-York Historical Society.*

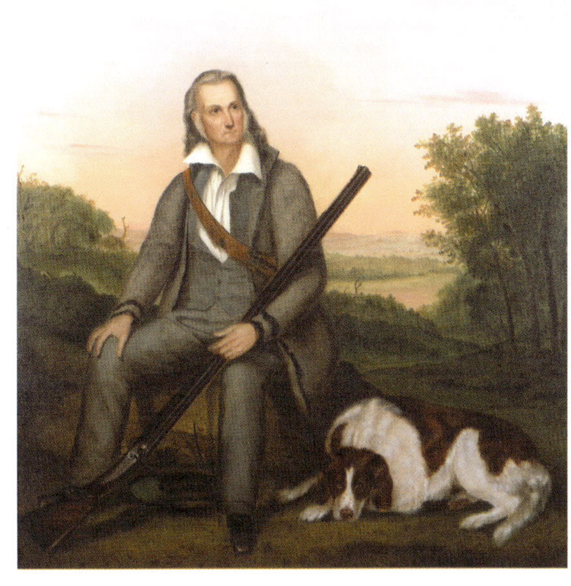

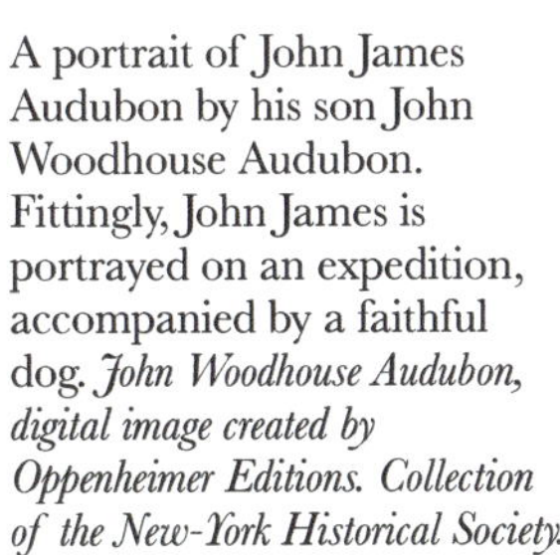

A portrait of John James Audubon by his son John Woodhouse Audubon. Fittingly, John James is portrayed on an expedition, accompanied by a faithful dog. *John Woodhouse Audubon, digital image created by Oppenheimer Editions. Collection of the New-York Historical Society.*

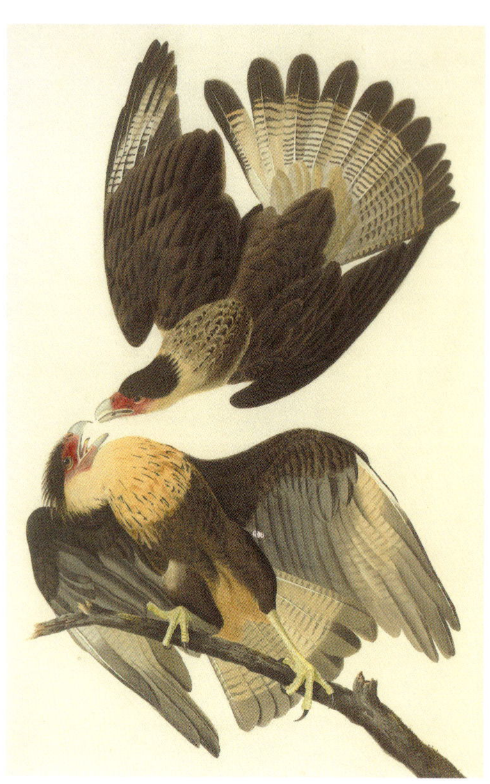

The crested caracara. This scene, painted at St. Augustine, shows two caracaras in combat. It exemplifies the motion, energy and liveliness Audubon was able to instill in his work. *John James Audubon, digital image created by Oppenheimer Editions. Collection of the New-York Historical Society.*

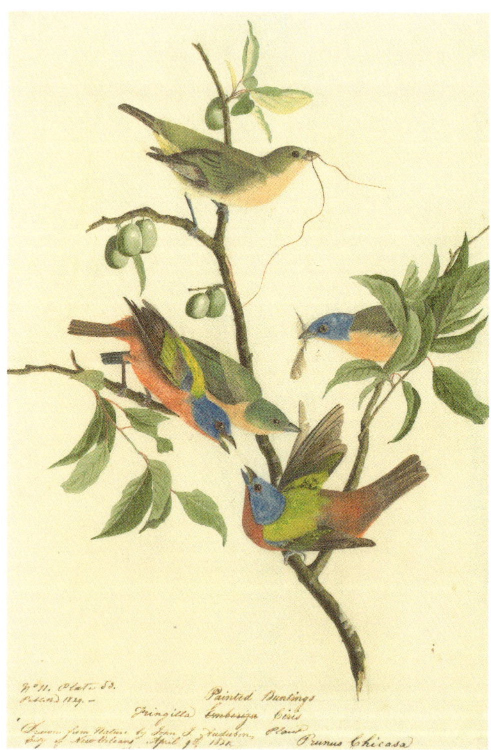

Audubon must have enjoyed the brilliant colors of the painted bunting, which he called the painted finch. *John James Audubon, digital image created by Oppenheimer Editions. Collection of the New-York Historical Society.*

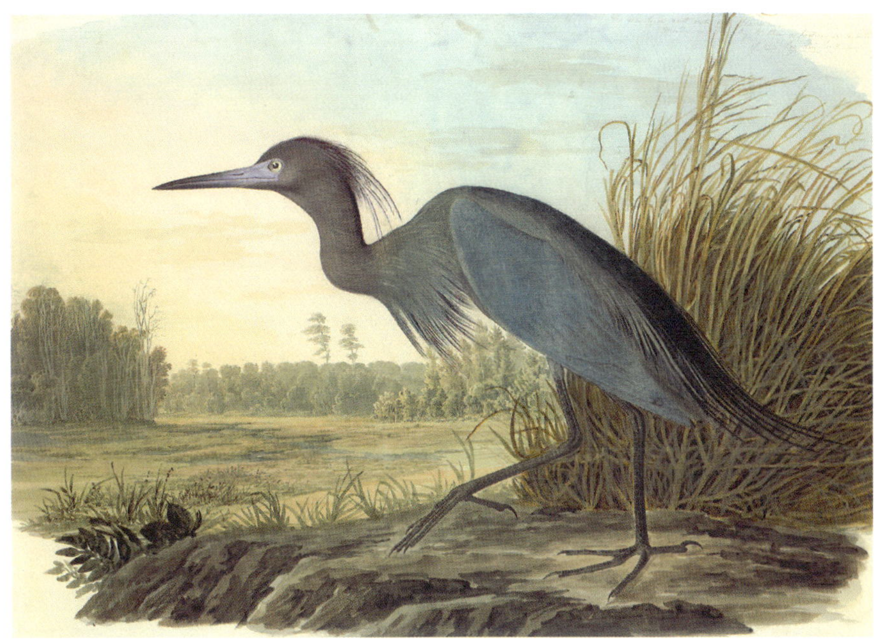

The little blue heron is a delicate creature, set in another fine landscape that evokes Audubon's treks through Florida. *John James Audubon, digital image created by Oppenheimer Editions. Collection of the New-York Historical Society.*

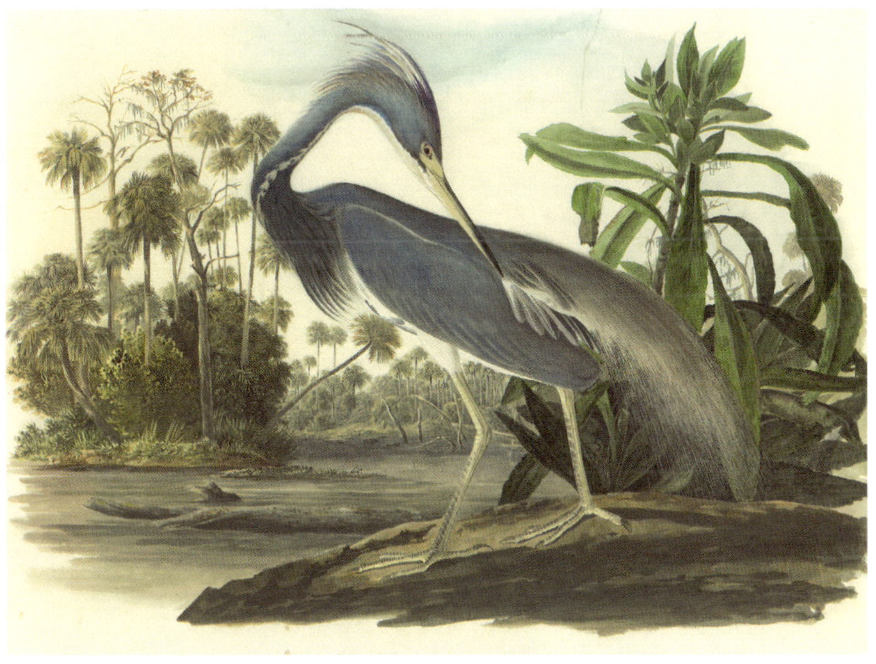

Audubon thought of the tricolored heron as the "Lady of the Waters." *John James Audubon, digital image created by Oppenheimer Editions. Collection of the New-York Historical Society.*

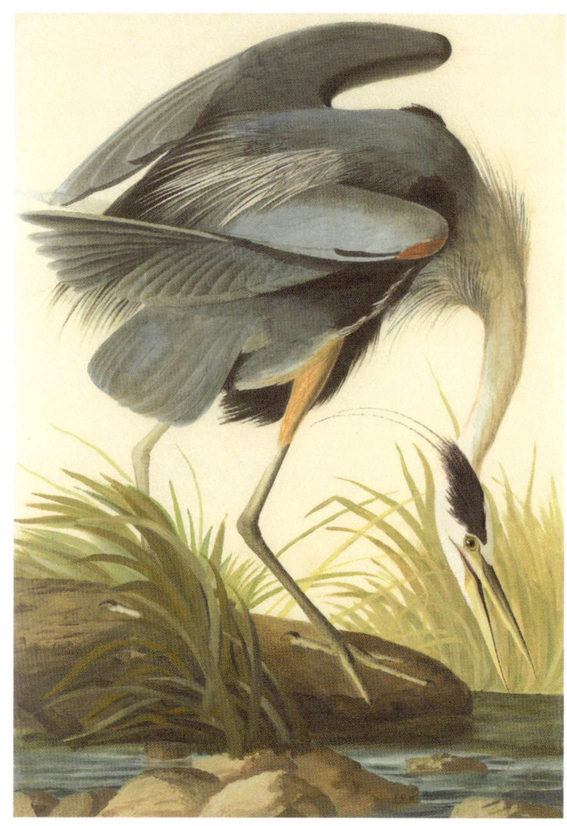

Left: The great blue heron seems ready to break through the frame and step into the reader's living room. *John James Audubon, digital image created by Oppenheimer Editions. Collection of the New-York Historical Society.*

Below: Audubon's portrayal of green herons also includes a highly accurate luna moth. *John James Audubon, digital image created by Oppenheimer Editions. Collection of the New-York Historical Society.*

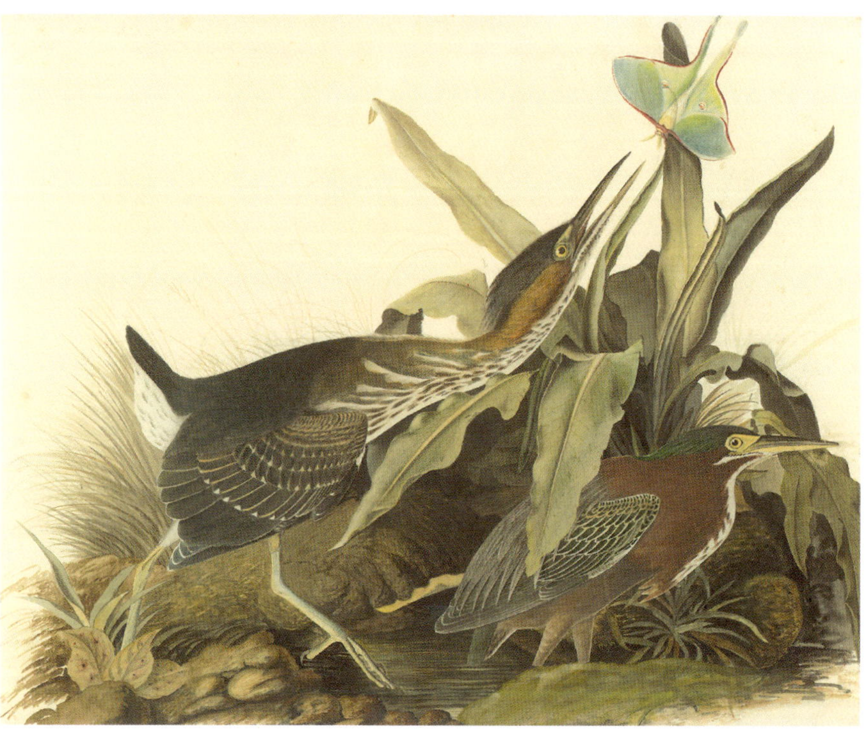

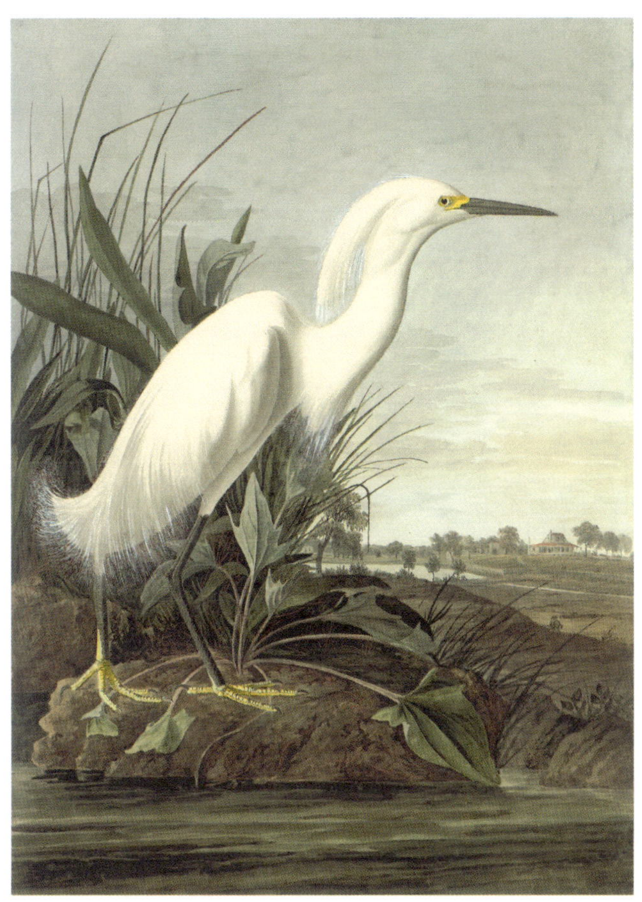

Left: The elegant forms of wading birds were always inspiring to Audubon's artistry, as this snowy egret shows. The landscape is a masterpiece in itself and portrays the richness of Florida's marshland and countryside. *John James Audubon, digital image created by Oppenheimer Editions. Collection of the New-York Historical Society.*

Below: Audubon observed numerous cormorants while in the Keys and believed that they were a distinct species that he called the "Florida cormorant." Today, this is identified as a double-crested cormorant. *John James Audubon, digital image created by Oppenheimer Editions. Collection of the New-York Historical Society.*

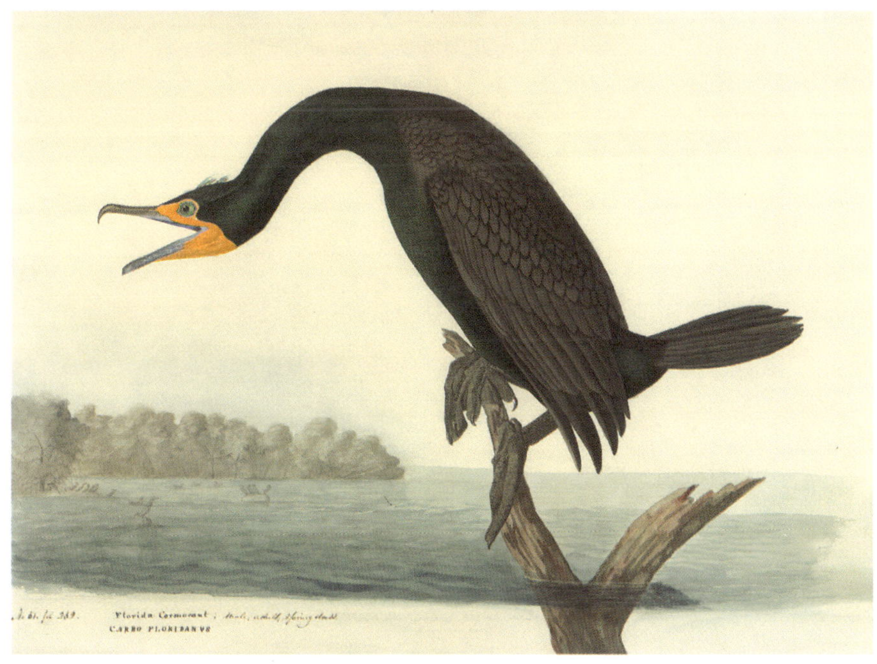

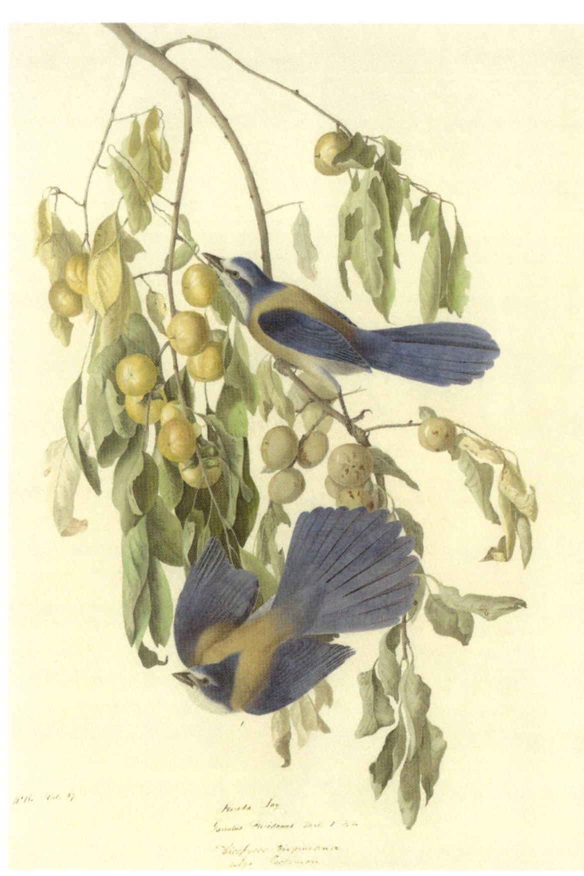

Left: A distinctive Florida species: the Florida scrub-jay. *John James Audubon, digital image created by Oppenheimer Editions. Collection of the New-York Historical Society.*

Below: The portrayal of the swallow-tailed kite shows Audubon's theatrical flair. *John James Audubon, digital image created by Oppenheimer Editions. Collection of the New-York Historical Society.*

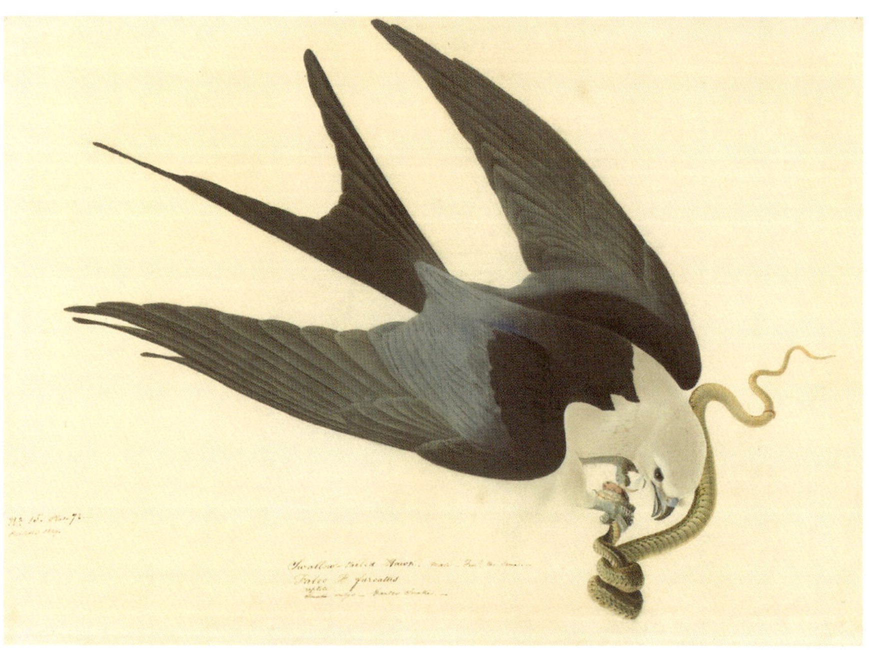

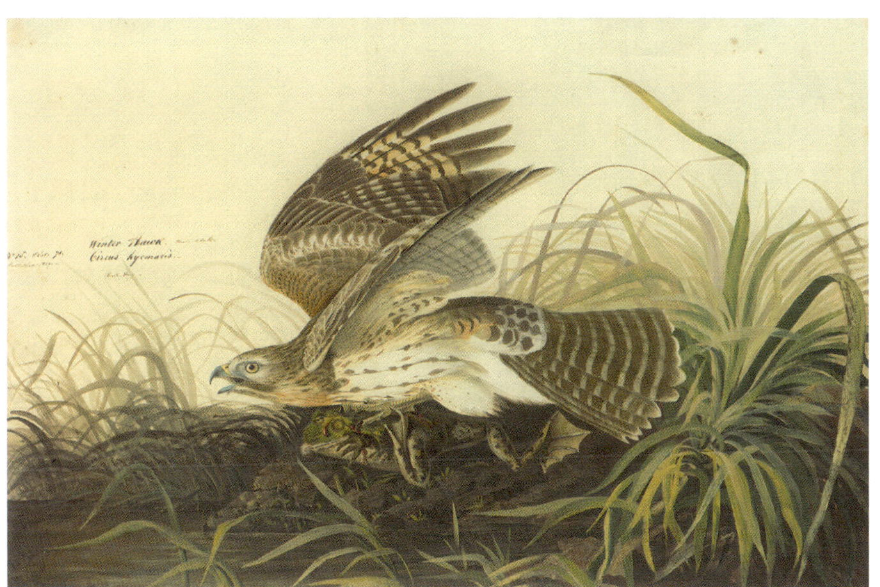

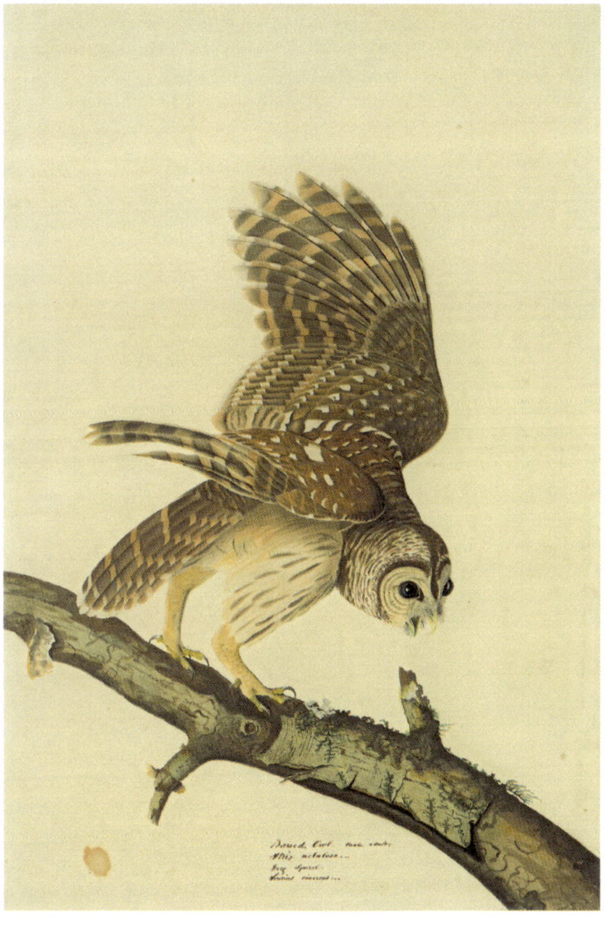

Above: Audubon mistook this juvenile red-shouldered hawk for a new species, which he named the "winter hawk." The error did not prevent him from finding inspiration for a dramatic work of art. *John James Audubon, digital image created by Oppenheimer Editions. Collection of the New-York Historical Society.*

Left: The barred owl looks as if it has soft feathers, and indeed it does. *John James Audubon, digital image created by Oppenheimer Editions. Collection of the New-York Historical Society.*

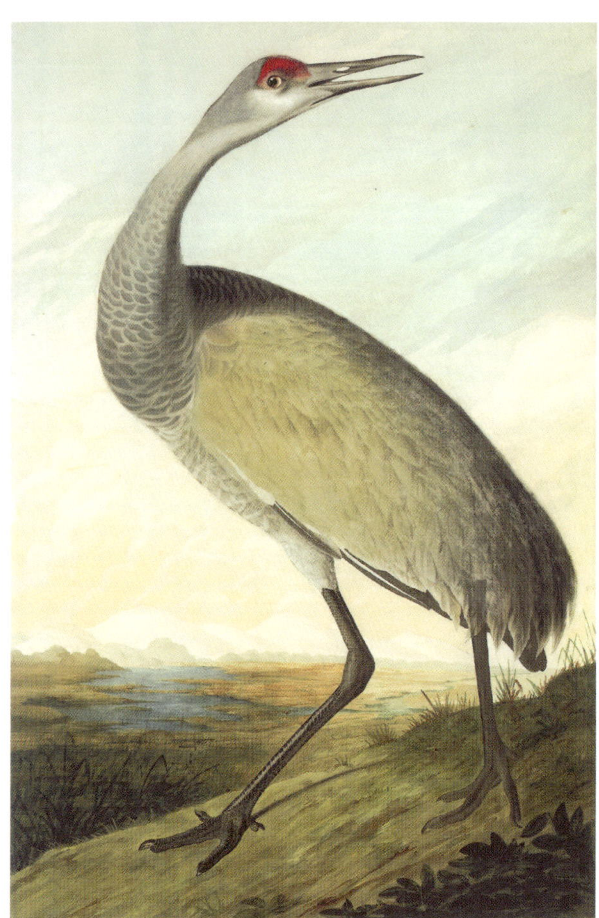

Left: A bright-eyed sandhill crane. *John James Audubon, digital image created by Oppenheimer Editions. Collection of the New-York Historical Society.*

Below: The roseate spoonbill, a colorful Florida species. Note that Audubon portrays the bird in breeding plumage, with a bright green head and golden tail feathers. The whimsical expression is more realistic than it might appear. *John James Audubon, digital image created by Oppenheimer Editions. Collection of the New-York Historical Society.*

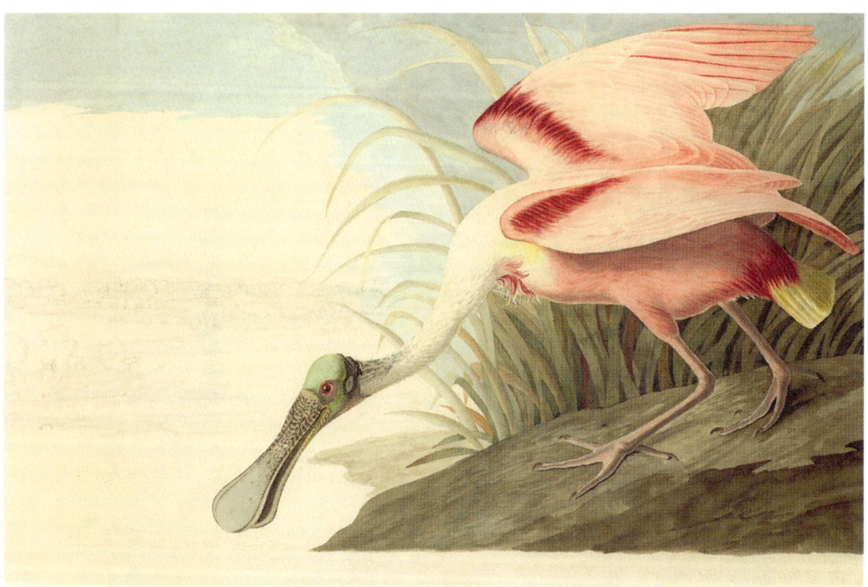

troubling or perhaps ironic today, especially since the Audubon Society is devoted to the protection of birds. However, it was a standard part of natural history studies at the time. Today, any natural history museum with roots in the nineteenth century or earlier has displays of specimens preserved through taxidermy. Audubon generally wrote about hunting and obtaining specimens in a matter-of-fact way. There are passages in his writing, however, wherein mixed feelings seem to surface. "How well do I remember the pain it gave me," he said of one occasion wherein he was shooting birds for this purpose. In another such passage, written while he was in Edinburgh, he looked back on his time in Florida and remembered shooting cormorants for the sake of illustrating them in *Birds of America*: "You must try to excuse these murders, dear reader, which in truth might not have been so numerous had I not thought of you quite as often while in the Florida Keys, with the burning sun over my head and my body oozing at every pore, as I do now while peaceably scratching my paper with an iron pen, in one of the comfortable and quite cool houses of Old Scotland." The expression "try to excuse these murders" was wry in its tone, but nevertheless, it dramatically shows feelings and regrets that Audubon often glossed over.

All other considerations aside, there is an artistic challenge to the nature artist working from specimens. True, the bird will not fly away, but neither is it alive. Recall that Mark Catesby used specimens only occasionally, preferring to paint birds from life. Although Audubon did use specimens, he realized that he needed to find a way to make them look as if they were still alive.

How did he achieve this? He developed a system of wiring to pose his specimens in a lifelike manner. This technique is considered a key to Audubon's success. The wired specimens led to sketches, the sketches led to watercolors and then, thanks to Havell and his studio, the watercolors led to the detailed color plates for *Birds of America*. Throughout the process, the sense of motion was retained; the image of the caracaras in combat is a great example of the dynamic style of Audubon's work.

Important though the system of wiring is, however, it alone does not explain the vitality that Audubon's birds seem to have. Essential complements were Audubon's experience and skill in observing birds in the wild. He brought to each work his memories of observation from life. The specimens were providing the realistic details of color and form, and the wiring system helped to provide a sense of motion, but it was Audubon's rich memories of adventure in the wilderness and the close observation of living birds that would allow him to rise above the limitations of working with specimens.

Just look at the eyes of his caracaras. Whereas German English nature artist Joseph Wolf had said that an artist who worked from specimens could never "know the true color of the eyes," the eyes of Audubon's caracaras are brilliant, reflective, limpid and active. Such vibrant and living eyes are to be seen in many of his bird portraits. This could not be achieved through taxidermy and wiring alone; this was something that Audubon was painting from memory. The sense of life that his birds have is one of Audubon's defining artistic attributes, and it is the fruitage of a lifetime of experience, observation and love.

12

"ELEGANCE AND GRACE"

Florida's Wading Birds

Audubon's reaction to Florida had not been one of love at first sight. Between trekking through storms and battling throngs of flying insects, his early expeditions in the state had been decidedly uncomfortable. In retrospect, there were some notable successes during this period—the dramatic image of the caracaras is clear evidence of that—but there is a querulous tone to Audubon's letters at the time. When he left for Charleston, South Carolina, it was by no means certain that he would ever return to Florida.

Yet return he did. Once again, he was aboard a navy ship—a cutter known as the *Marion*, on which he sailed to the Florida Keys. Audubon enjoyed his time aboard the *Marion* and wrote amiably of "her gallant officers and the brave tars who formed her crew." In fact, in comparison to his disconsolate perspective on the St. John's River, Audubon sounds like a new man on this voyage. His sense of adventure had returned, and he was excited by the new places that he was exploring.

As the *Marion* approached the inlet of Indian Key, having successfully avoided the perils of a coral reef, Audubon recalled: "We found ourselves in safe anchoring ground, within a few furlongs of the land. The next moment saw the oars of a boat propelling us towards the shore, and in brief time we stood on the desired beach. With what delightful feelings did we gaze on the objects around us!—the gorgeous flowers, the singular and beautiful plants, the luxuriant trees. The balmy air which we breathed filled us with animation, so pure and salubrious did it seem to be." This is a far cry from complaints about muddy socks.

Of course, glimpses of bird life were a major reason for his excitement. Audubon's first impression of the birds of the Keys both reflects and magnifies his own sense of joy: "The birds which we saw were almost all new to us; their lovely forms appeared to be arrayed in more brilliant apparel than I had ever before seen, and as they gambolled in happy playfulness among the bushes, or glided over the light green waters, we longed to form a more intimate acquaintance with them." The works of art inspired by this voyage would more than justify this early promise.

HERONS IN THE KEYS

Among the beautiful birds that Audubon saw in the Keys were several kinds of herons. The elegant forms of wading birds always inspired him, and their portraits are rightly among the most renowned of his works of art.

Consider the little blue heron, which Audubon observed nesting in the Keys. In his writing, he described how this heron can be seen "quietly and in silence walking along the margins of the water, with an elegance and grace which can never fail to please." These qualities are clearly evident in Audubon's portrait of the bird, which is in profile. It is a calm image, and the combative caracaras of St. Augustine seem frenetic by comparison. On the other hand, the little blue heron does not have the stillness of the pelicans. Instead, Audubon gives this image a sense of quiet motion. The bird is in the midst of walking; one foot is firmly on the ground, and the other foot is raised up. The delicacy of movement is extraordinary; you just know that even if you were standing right in front of the heron, you would never hear its footfalls.

The use of color is also important, and when considered within the body of Audubon's work, it shows the artist's adaptability to the colors of his subjects. In an upcoming chapter, we will look at the roseate spoonbill and see how Audubon used flamboyant color when the plumage of a bird called for it. For the little blue heron, on the other hand, he uses a palette that combines minimalism with flashes of richness, effectively conveying the natural colors of this bird. The plumage is a charcoal gray in places, but this subdued color gives way to deep blues and purples. The tip of the beak is black, but the mid and upper beak is bluish-purple, as is the area around the eyes; thus, the brilliant yellow of the eye makes for a striking contrast.

The background of the little blue heron portrait is a beautiful example of Audubon's skill as a landscape painter. The setting is not that of the Keys, but it is certainly evocative of a Floridian marsh. The richness of the environment is very apparent. So, too, is Audubon's mastery of perspective. Tufts of grass near the heron's feet, and a large clump of tall grasses just behind it, appear very close to the viewer. Beyond is an open marshland that narrows in the distance, bordered by forest. The illusion of three-dimensionality in painting is a mark of artistic skill that has been prized since the days of the Italian Renaissance. For Audubon's purposes, this sense of perspective also has another advantage: it enhances our impression that the bird in the foreground really is right in front of us.

A spectacular landscape is found in Audubon's image of the tricolored heron. Here, the backdrop is a lush swamp dotted with palm trees. Audubon's intention is likely to show the bayous of Louisiana, where he spent considerable time and where he also observed this species; in fact, he called it the "Louisiana Heron." However, his written description invites the reader to imagine its motion as "it leisurely walks over the pure sand beaches of the coast of Florida, arrayed in the full beauty of its spring plumage." He mentions the "glossy tints," that is, the iridescent feathers, and the "tempered hues" of its wings. Audubon's portrait does indeed highlight the richness and varied colors of the feathers, which are celebrated by the heron's current name. "Delicate in form, beautiful in plumage, and graceful in its movements, I never see this interesting Heron, without calling it the Lady of the Waters." Surely, "Lady of the Waters" would be an apt title for his portrait of the tricolored heron; grace is nearly always an essential feature of Audubon's images of wading birds.

The action-oriented composition that he used to portray the great blue heron, however, is an exception. Here, the enormous bird is about to spear a fish; its neck is curved in an uncomfortable-looking posture as its beak plunges toward the water. The composition is arresting and dramatic, very different from the air of tranquility that Audubon usually brings to his portrayals of waders. The artist's skill with action scenes and his ingenuity in devising varied compositions for his bird portraits might be motivations here; however, there is also a more pressing reason for the great blue heron's posture.

A curious aspect of *Birds of America* was that one of Audubon's initial goals was to have all of the images be life-size. This is easily forgotten today, because we are used to seeing Audubon's artwork in a variety of sizes. In its original form, however, the book was enormous. Each illustration measured more than two feet by three feet. Still, it was a challenge to fit in a life-size image of a bird as large as the great blue heron. If it looks like Audubon's great blue heron is bending over to fit into the frame—well, yes, that's exactly what it is doing.

As a side point, this also explains Audubon's strange lack of success with hummingbirds. He wrote about the ruby-throated hummingbird very poetically, and it is a passage wherein Audubon manifests a spiritual aspect to his appreciation of nature: "I ask of you, kind reader, who, on observing this glittering fragment of the rainbow, would not pause, admire, and instantly turn his mind with reverence toward the Almighty Creator, the wonders of whose hand we at every step discover?" Just the phrase "glittering fragment of the rainbow" makes one eager to see Audubon's picture of the hummingbirds; however, it is the rare instance where the picture might prompt puzzlement rather than admiration. There are numerous hummingbirds in the image, and they are shown in different phases of motion; however, within the composition, they are all so small that they seem overshadowed by the flowers and leaves. It appears to be a missed opportunity, and a rather obvious one at that; surely if Audubon had zoomed in on the birds, then their iridescent feathers, which he wrote about so poetically, could be better displayed. In fact, it is not that the artist simply failed to think of this; rather, he was limited by the concept of presenting each species as life-size. Thus, birds as varied as the great blue heron and the ruby-throated hummingbird were shown to scale—even if the heron looks a bit like a contortionist and the hummingbirds seem lost in the vegetation.

Along with the great blue, Audubon observed another enormous heron while he was in the Keys—the great white heron, a bird distinct to Florida. Today, the classification of the great white heron is a matter of some debate. It has been considered a regional color morph of the great blue heron, but there are arguments for declaring it a subspecies or a separate species. Understandably, Audubon viewed the great blue and the great white as two different species. He noted that the great white herons were constant residents of the Keys and that they were especially abundant there during the breeding season. As with the great blue, it was a struggle for him to get this large bird into the frame. Audubon portrayed the great white heron with its head rising from the water, a fish in its beak, its body still in a crouching posture. Even so, the tips of the beak and the back edge of one foot are cut off by the frame.

From the Watercolors to the Book

The plumage in these heron portraits, especially those of the little blue and the tricolored, show the skill of Audubon's brushstrokes. This is where viewing the original watercolors, instead of just the plates, is of such value. The watercolors bring us closer to a glimpse of Audubon's own hand, without the intervening logistics of printing. Furthermore, the watercolors represent a key intermediate portion of the artistic process.

Once Audubon had used his taxidermy skills and his inventive system of wiring to pose bird specimens in a lifelike way, he would then sketch the specimens; the sketches, in turn, would become the basis for his watercolor paintings. This system allowed Audubon flexibility and meant that he did not have to carry hundreds of stuffed birds in his luggage wherever he traveled.

The watercolors, therefore, have great value in combining the immediacy of field sketches along with the careful composition of finished works of art. Today, they allow the viewer to more fully appreciate Audubon as an artist and specifically as a fine painter. For example, a close look at the plumage of the little blue heron reveals the delicacy of Audubon's brushstrokes. Likewise, the marshy waters of the bayou behind the tricolored heron suggest the graceful motion of the artist's brush.

These paintings are beautiful in themselves. For them to be essentially transformed into a massive, illustrated book, however, Audubon needed Havell and his London studio. This is where the contacts that he had established in London were essential. The scale of the project was monumental: the finished book would consist of four leather-bound volumes with a total of some four hundred color images. The images were made via a process known as aquatinting, which required painstaking effort and expertise but allowed for wonderfully vivid color. And in keeping with Audubon's desire for the birds to be portrayed at life-size, or as close to it as possible, the book was monumental. This first edition of *Birds of America* would be given a nickname appropriate to its scale, although ironically mammalian rather than avian: the Double Elephant Folio.

Considerable manpower, well beyond the efforts of Audubon himself, went into all this. Havell ran his studio in partnership with his father, and they employed about fifty people. *Birds of America* was a great achievement for the studio. It was essential to Audubon's success that he had found the talent, and the enthusiasm, that Havell and his crew represented. The enthusiasm can hardly be overrated. This was not just a business venture for Havell;

it was a project that changed his life. He was so inspired by Audubon's artwork and stories of adventure that after the book was finished, he actually immigrated to the New World himself. There, he began publishing North American landscape scenes.

Green Heron and Snowy Heron

Audubon also painted beautiful portraits of the green heron and the snowy egret. In his day, the snowy egret was known as the snowy heron—understandably given the similarities in form among these waders. Viewed in connection with his other images of wading birds, and for that matter with his entire body of work, these two images are great examples of the variety that is to be found in Audubon's art. As Audubon himself was well aware, this is a reflection of the boundless variety of the natural world.

Of course, each bird is different, and many of Audubon's predecessors would have relied on that to provide interest. Audubon, skilled though he is at visually explaining the differences between species, does not rely on those differences to keep the work from appearing repetitive. Instead, he imaginatively uses rich landscapes, as we have seen, along with varied elements of composition. Thus, even setting aside ornithology, each image is a unique work of art. In the category of Florida waders, most portraits convey the elegance and grace that Audubon appreciated in these birds, yet each portrait is unique.

Look at the green heron image, and you will see an element that we have not encountered before. Along with the green herons (a pair of them), the scene includes a luna moth, which one of the herons is trying to catch and eat. Audubon provides a realistic and detailed image of this large and colorful insect. The shape of the wings is unmistakable—in modern times, the luna moth could serve as the inspiration for a science fiction writer imagining an alien spaceship. The use of color is brilliant—Audubon shows the range of greens on the luna moth, from key lime to seafoam. The eyespots on the wings and even the fluffy antennae are portrayed with great accuracy.

Is Audubon an artist of birds or insects? His focus was on birds, but this image shows that his skills could be applied to lepidoptera as well. The luna moth does not have to be there, of course; Audubon has chosen to include the exotic-looking creature to add interest and variety. The choice also shows artistry of color, because the light greens of the luna moth are both contrasting and complementary to the deeper greens (and the purples) of the herons' plumage. This painting is also of interest because all three of the artists considered in this book—Mark Catesby, William Bartram and John James Audubon—portrayed the green heron, each in his own way.

As for the snowy egret portrait, it features one of Audubon's wonderfully rich Floridian landscapes, with a marshy foreground and a line of trees along the distant horizon. It also has an architectural element—another trick that Audubon would use to make his scenes varied and interesting. A ranch can be seen in the distance, with barns and outbuildings as well as a stately gray house with a large verandah and sloping red rooflines. It is beautifully situated among tall trees and near the shores of a small body of water. This is not a wilderness scene but a countryside one. It brings in a comforting theme of home.

Placing the egret in such a setting is quite accurate—even in the much more highly developed conditions of today, one does not have to go out into the wilderness to see egrets in Florida. The work of art might also be a grand reminder that the wonders of nature can be found close to home. The snowy egret is a beautiful creature: Audubon's painting shows the bird's splendid white plumes, like the feathers on a knight's helmet, as well as the striking color contrast. The feet are a bold yellow, as is the area of the face around the eyes; these details are very accurate, and they also play off, with great artistry, against the bright white feathers. The bird is in profile, so we see only one eye, but that eye is amazing. It is a slightly lighter yellow than the flamboyant color that immediately surrounds it, and it is staring out at us. Perhaps by placing this creature near someone's home, Audubon is reminding us that even if we are not able to follow his footsteps out into the wilderness, there are still treasures that we can discover in the natural world. Given Florida's varied and abundant bird life, that is still true today.

13

ACROBATIC TERNS AND JOYOUS CORMORANTS

The Dry Tortugas and the Keys

Audubon's success in the Keys was followed by a trip to the Dry Tortugas. Still aboard the *Marion*, he risked the perils of coral reefs and potential shipwreck to visit these small islands, where he was rewarded with sights of amazing seabirds.

Visitors to the Dry Tortugas today usually get there by ferry or seaplane, with Key West as their starting point. These islands are made of sand and coral, and they are devoid of fresh water—thus the name "Dry." Establishing "Dry" as part of the name meant that a sailor studying a chart would be warned that he would not be able to replenish water supplies there. Today, the Dry Tortugas are a national park, and the park rangers who are stationed there still make use of a nineteenth-century system for catching rainwater; they also use a desalination unit to make seawater potable. The other part of the name, "Tortugas," is Spanish for "turtles." This name was given to the islands by their discoverer, Ponce de Leon, who found that sea turtles were abundant near their shores.

Modern visitors admire a historic fortress, known as Fort Jefferson, as well as a lighthouse. Both structures date from the nineteenth century. However, when Audubon visited in 1832, the fortress did not yet exist; construction would not begin until nearly fifteen years later. There was a lighthouse there—a fairly new structure that had been in use for just a few years. Theoretically, that made Audubon's voyage safer. The coral reefs near the Dry Tortugas had claimed many ships, and the purpose of the lighthouse was to help guide mariners around such perils. However, it did not prove adequate, and the shipwrecks continued for decades, until a more effective lighthouse (the one that can be seen today) was built in the 1850s.

Thankfully, the captain and crew of the *Marion* were able to avoid the perilous reefs. The lighthouse of their day, despite its shortcomings, might have been a help; Audubon's account would mention "the light-house lantern…a bright gem glittering in the rays of the sun." The islands of the Dry Tortugas are still of great interest to birdwatchers today, and Audubon considered his trip to be highly worthwhile.

Abundance of Seabirds

Audubon vividly recalled his first sight of the islands. He was standing on the deck of the *Marion*. The weather was "very beautiful, although hot," and the winds favorable. From a young lad on the rigging, the cry of "Land!" was heard. "It was the low keys of the Tortugas, toward which we had been steering."

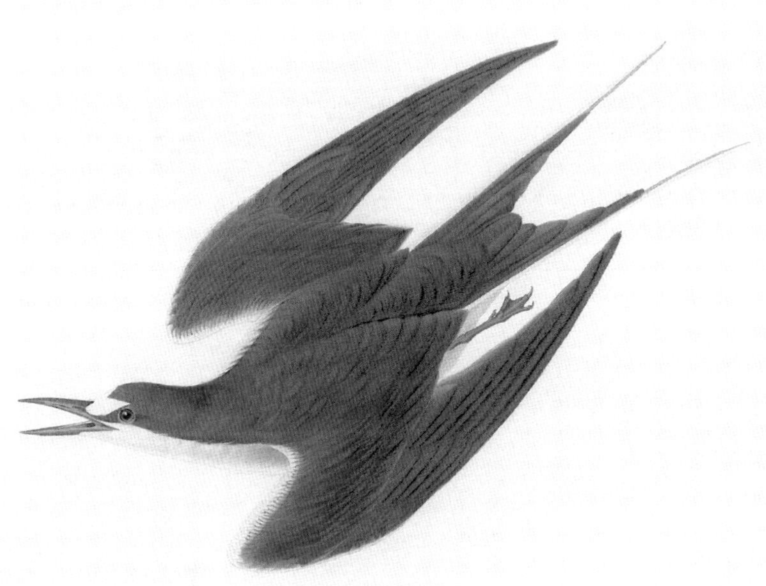

A voyage to the Dry Tortugas led to Audubon's observation of the sooty tern. *Digital image created by Oppenheimer Editions. Collection of the New-York Historical Society.*

Audubon's curiosity was piqued by the first lieutenant's description of the vast numbers of seabirds that could be found nesting there at that time of year. "Before we cast anchor," he promised, "you will see them rise in swarms like those of bees when disturbed in their hive, and their cries will deafen you."

He was right. As Audubon eagerly scanned the islands, he soon saw what looked like a cloud rising from one of them. It was a cloud of birds. When Audubon landed, the birds so filled the surrounding air that, for a moment, he thought that they would lift him up off the ground. The impression is a great testament both to the bird population and to the artist's active imagination. The image that it suggests, of John James Audubon being borne aloft on a cloud of birds, is memorable in itself.

These numerous seabirds included brown noddies, brown boobies and sooty terns. All of these were species that Audubon would have been unlikely to see if he had stayed on the mainland. They are true seabirds whose winged voyages across the world's oceans can take on epic proportions. Consider the sooty tern and some of its relatives. Audubon was fascinated by terns, but even he only knew the tip of the iceberg when it comes to how amazing they are.

Voyages in the Sky

The sooty tern was called the "black and white swallow" by the friendly lieutenant of the *Marion*, but many sailors have called it the "wide-awake" because of its long flights. Young sooty terns might spend two to five years at sea before returning to the breeding grounds of the Dry Tortugas; much of that time is spent aloft. They live in the air. It is no wonder that sailors called them wide-awakes. Some scientists today believe that seabirds that make such long flights are actually able to sleep in the air, and that somehow only one hemisphere of the brain sleeps at a time.

Appreciation for the extraordinary aerial lives of such birds can also be gained by considering a related tern species, the Arctic tern. They can sometimes be spotted off the coast of Florida during their migrations. Audubon encountered this species, not while he was here in Florida but in a place that must have seemed a world away—a group of islands between Nova Scotia and Labrador. His description of Arctic terns provides insight into his literary style: "Light as a sylph, the Arctic Tern dances through the air above and around you. The graces, one might imagine, had taught it to perform those beautiful gambols which you see it display the moment you approach the spot which it has chosen for its nest." In the fashion of his time, he was using classical allusions to enhance the poetic flair of his writing. Furthermore, his description of the journeys of the terns shows that he knew they traveled through both frigid and tropical climates: "Now over some solitary green isle, a creek or an extensive bay, it sweeps, now over the expanse of the boundless sea; at length it has reached the distant regions of the north, and amidst the floating icebergs stoops to pick up a shrimp. It betakes itself to the borders of a lonely sand-bank, or a low rocky island." Finally, he complements the literary tone of this passage with a touch of anthropomorphism: "There side by side the males and the females alight, and congratulate each other on the happy termination of their long journey."

However, Audubon's most fascinating statement regarding Arctic terns is perhaps this one: "Over many a league of ocean has it passed, regardless of the dangers and difficulties that might deter a more considerate [cautious] traveller." Clearly, he knew that these birds made great migrations. Yet he would have been even more amazed if he had realized the full extent of their flights. This has been discovered using modern tracking methods—high-tech versions of the silver thread. A single Arctic tern can, during its lifetime, travel a distance equivalent of three or four round trips to the moon. Their migration between the Arctic and the Antarctic is fifty-six thousand miles long—"many a league," to be sure—and somehow, they know how to take advantage of the prevailing winds and correlate that with their direction.

Fittingly, then, the majority of Audubon's tern images emphasize motion; this is in keeping with their great migrations, and it also conveys the acrobatic nature of their flights. The sooty tern is shown in a horizontal view, soaring through the sky with a slightly downward trajectory. The wings are pulled back and the streamlined shape is very clear. The bird is probably about to make one of its spectacular dives. The Arctic tern is shown in mid-dive, with a vertical format to the composition. Terns can dive through the air at very high speed, from thirty feet or more above the water, and then change direction at the last minute to skim above the waves and catch fish that are near the surface. A still image cannot literally show this motion, but Audubon used all his skills to strongly suggest it. Although his terns are frozen in an instant of time, their quick and acrobatic behavior is unmistakable.

The plumage of terns is black, white and gray, and Audubon, who loved color, must have occasionally tired of this palette. Compare his portrayal of the bird he called the painted finch, which is known today as the painted bunting. There, Audubon got to use vibrant blues, yellows, greens and reds. To heighten the glistening hues of the cobalt blue, he mixed it with a hint of white—an artist's trick to make a bright color even brighter. Audubon wanted to convey the brilliant plumage that makes the painted bunting so beautiful, and he probably enjoyed working with bright colors. In fact, for bird species that lack bright plumage, like the terns, he would sometimes go out of his way to include features in the landscape or environment that would provide splashes of color. For example, in his image of the royal tern, he shows the bird standing on a beach next to a red crab.

For the portrait of the sooty tern, however, he maintains a subtle palette, placing the tern in mid-air against a clouded sky. Patches of very pale blue in the sky, some pink for the bird's mouth and brown for its irises add touches of color, but most of the composition is monochromatic. This is an interesting variation in Audubon's style. The minimalist approach enhances the importance of linear elements like the streamlined wings and the forked tail. This heightens the sense of aerodynamic motion—essential to the lives of terns and to the success of this work of art. Audubon was a flamboyant man and a flamboyant artist, but he knew how to use a minimalist style when it fit with a bird and a theme.

"A JOYOUS MULTITUDE"

Cormorants in the Keys

It was in the Keys that Audubon visited great colonies of double-crested cormorants. He considered the southern population of the double-crested cormorant as a separate species that he named the "Florida cormorant," although the classification and name are no longer accepted. One of his visits to a cormorant colony was as a member of a group that included a guide named James Egan. The local knowledge that Egan—a Bahamian who had lived in southern Florida for some three decades—provided was of great value to Audubon. Audubon called the guide "a man of great judgment, sagacity, and integrity." Besides, he was fascinated by the way Egan had once kept a great white heron as a kind of semi-tamed outdoor pet. As the enthusiastic visitor and the shrewd longtime resident, Audubon and Egan must have been an interesting pair. Their approach to the cormorant colony was a characteristically Floridian scene: they were piloting a small boat through a mangrove swamp on a ninety-degree day when they saw thousands of nesting cormorants.

Another occasion came when Audubon was "rambling over one of the Keys" by himself. He came to the entrance of a channel of water into another mangrove swamp. He looked at the water and noticed that fish were abundant; this convinced him that there were no sharks nearby, and he decided to begin wading. His curiosity was soon piqued by "curious sounds," which he followed. "The sounds were loud and constantly renewed, as if they came from a joyous multitude." They proved to be the sounds of cormorants. Audubon had found another colony. Here, many of the birds were in the midst of courtship. As he would put it, with one of his endearingly human descriptions, "they were engaged in going through their nuptial ceremonies." Each couple would "swim joyously around each other, croaking all the while."

These experiences inform Audubon's portrait of his Florida cormorant. As usual, the focus is on a single bird; however, in the background, the shapes of numerous additional cormorants can be seen. Some are standing on rocks or on the shore, while others are in flight. The background also includes a line of low green trees near the water—mangroves. A comparison of the watercolor that Audubon painted and the image that appeared in *Birds of America* underscores the important role that Robert Havell played. In the plate, there are more trees visible, and the root structure is more elaborate, positively identifying them as mangroves. Such additions were based on Audubon's sketches and his written instructions; he had more experience with mangroves than the London artist did.

As for the cormorant in the foreground, Audubon shows it poised on a dead branch that is jutting out from the water; the bird is leaning forward so that the curvature of its long neck is displayed. With the bird itself, there is another important difference between the watercolor and the plate. The plate in *Birds of America* highlights the iridescent green hues of the cormorant's neck, whereas the plumage in the watercolor is mostly black. Much of the difference would depend on the lighting and the angle of the observer. The accompanying written description notes: "All the silky part of the plumage is greenish-black, at a distance appearing black, but at hand in a strong light green." The decision to emphasize the green for the image in the book adds richness. Such changes exemplify the active artistic partnership that Audubon and Havell cultivated.

With loud and joyful colonies of cormorants, several varieties of beautiful herons and champions of long-distance flying such as the terns, there is no doubt that Audubon found many reasons to be thankful that he visited the islands off the tip of southern Florida. His voyages to the Keys and the Dry Tortugas gave him the observation and inspiration for triumphantly beautiful avian portraits.

14

SCRUB-JAYS AND BIRDS OF PREY

Treasure Hunting in Florida

It is a historical curiosity that Audubon knew about the salvage of shipwrecks on the Florida coast, and he even met some salvagers—"Wreckers," as they were then known. This was not quite the salvage work that we know today, with expert divers in the tradition of Mel Fisher researching the voyages of the Spanish galleons and finding treasures of gold, silver and emeralds. The wreckers Audubon met were in search of recent shipwrecks, which coral reefs like those near the Dry Tortugas amply provided for them.

Audubon at first thought that wreckers would be a danger to his voyage; he pictured them as pirates. "Long before I reached the lovely islets that border the south-eastern shores of the Floridas, the accounts I had heard of 'The Wreckers' had deeply prejudiced me against them. Often had I been informed of the cruel and cowardly methods which it was alleged they employ to allure vessels of all nations to the dreaded reefs, that they might plunder their cargoes, and rob their crews and passengers of their effects." He associated these men with "piratical depredation, barbarous usage, and even murder." The wreckers he met, however, seemed to be friendly, courteous and peaceable. They even gave him a collection of birds' eggs when they learned of the reasons for his travels in Florida.

Whether the search is for recent cargoes or Spanish doubloons, the work of salvagers has long been a part of Florida's history. Audubon, however, was here looking for treasures of a different kind. Some additional examples of his paintings of Florida birds will provide further evidence for the success of his personal treasure hunt.

The Florida Jay—A Wine Connoisseur?

Audubon recognized the Florida scrub-jay, which he called simply the "Florida Jay," as a distinctive species. "This beautiful and lively bird is a constant resident in the south-western parts of Florida, from which country it seldom if ever removes to any great distance." In describing the range of the species, he took the opportunity to point out an error made by Charles Lucien Bonaparte, who claimed it was found as far from Florida as Kentucky. "We believe that he has been misinformed," said Audubon dryly, pleased, it seems, to have the opportunity to contradict Bonaparte. Audubon described the Florida scrub-jay's quick flight, its hopping motion and its omnivorous diet. "Its notes are softer than those of its relative the blue jay," he wrote; of course, blue jays are very loud indeed for their size.

For the portrait, he showed two scrub-jays in a persimmon tree. The tail of one is outspread, emphasizing the rich blue as well as the beauty of the individual feathers. The other one can be seen perching, its feet curled around the branch with fine detail. The Florida scrub-jay is in fact so comfortable in this position that researchers who are carrying on Audubon's tradition of bird banding today will often give scrub-jays a pencil to curl their feet around while the band is being put in place.

Audubon also told a curious story about a pair of Florida scrub-jays being kept as pets—a practice that would not be countenanced today. "They were in full plumage, and extremely beautiful. The male was often observed to pay very particular attentions to the female, at the approach of spring. They were fed upon rice, and all kinds of dried fruit." These scrub-jays had the cleverness of the corvid family to which, like crows and ravens, they belong. And it seems that they had refined taste. In the evenings, their cage would be opened, and they would promptly fly over to the dining table, where they enjoyed almonds. They were also given claret—dry red winc from France—which they drank. The claret was diluted with water; nevertheless, it seems that the adaptability of these birds had extended to developing a taste for wine.

An Intrepid Kite

The swallow-tailed kite, as Audubon painted it, has a decidedly theatrical quality. In that respect, it recalls his image of the caracaras, yet in other ways, it can be compared to his portrayal of the sooty tern. Really, the swallow-tailed kite portrait is a fusion of various aspects of Audubon's style and probably his personality. Audubon writes of observing this species in Louisiana; thus, his image of the bird was not dependent upon his travels in Florida. However, it does give us a memorable portrayal of a species that is very familiar in Florida today.

First, consider the theatricality. The kite has caught a snake, grasping its head in one talon. The reptile's mouth is open, as if it is trying to strike out at the bird with its fangs but is unable to do so; the forked tongue trails off into the air. The long body is curled and in places seems almost knotted. The kite is staring intently at its prey and seems ready to strike with its beak to deliver a coup-de-grace. The dramatic impression of a duel to the death with a snake might remind a modern audience of Rudyard Kipling's heroic mongoose story "Rikki-Tikki-Tavi." To bring the impression back to Audubon's own experience, however, recall that he had learned to fence during his youth in France and that he was a skillful enough swordsman to earn money by giving lessons. Perhaps the impression of a duel that Audubon could bring to such images—swallow-tailed kite versus snake, caracara versus caracara—was informed by his knowledge and experience of fencing.

At the same time, there is an aspect of this painting that recalls the portrait of the sooty tern. For that image, Audubon used the minimalist colors of the tern to enhance the sense of motion. That technique is used here as well. The swallow-tailed kite is basically monochromatic. The plumage is black and white with a range of charcoal tones, while the talons and the beak show dove gray hues. Of course, this is the nature of the bird's plumage, but it is significant that the background is entirely bare. The kite seems to have flown across a blank page or an empty canvas. The lack of background is quite unusual for Audubon, and this stark composition emphasizes the simplicity of the kite's colors. Our attention is drawn to the linear elements and therefore to the suggestion of speed. With the sweeping lines of its forked tail and curved wings, Audubon's swallow-tailed kite becomes a study in geometry and motion, a marvel of natural engineering—and from the snake's perspective, a deadly missile.

This choice of artistic emphasis is in keeping with Audubon's observations of the swallow-tailed kite, which he called the swallow-tailed hawk: "It moves through the air with such ease and grace, that it is impossible for any individual, who takes the least pleasure in observing the manners of birds, not to be delighted by the sight of it whilst on wing….Their motions are astonishingly rapid, and the deep curves which they describe, their sudden doublings and crossings, and the extreme ease with which they seem to cleave the air, excite the admiration." Such impressions of speed and agility in flight were aptly conveyed in the watercolor painting and the subsequent image for *Birds of America*.

Fascination with the dynamic flying abilities of kites has a noble history in art. Leonardo da Vinci observed European species of kite during his natural history expeditions in the hills of Tuscany. By watching and sketching them, he hoped to discover the secret of flight. In his *Codex on the Flight of Birds*, Leonardo wrote about the way a kite can descend through the air with increasing speed, "flying without flapping its wings." Audubon's portrait of the swallow-tailed kite, with its streamlined form, shows just such a motion—a triumph of engineering in nature.

The Winter Hawk—An Audubon Error

For all his skill as an observer, Audubon did make mistakes. Leaving aside the storytelling and character-creation that were part of his American Woodsman persona, there are a few definite ornithological errors in Audubon's work, along with some puzzling "mystery birds." Oftentimes, when he made mistakes, it was because his enthusiasm got the best of him—a weakness that came along with his virtues. Audubon could get so excited about discovering a new species that he missed the fact that it wasn't really new—or he convinced himself that it was.

An infamous example is the immature bald eagle that he mistook for an entirely new eagle species. He happily named it the "bird of Washington" out of admiration for George, and his portrait of it, a dignified profile view, does have a suggestion of stalwart leadership. Evidently, Audubon did not know that immature bald eagles do not have the distinctive white-feathered head.

He made the same type of mistake with the red-shouldered hawk, a bird of prey commonly seen in Florida. Here, too, Audubon mistook an immature individual for a separate species. He named this purported species the "winter hawk." In this case, however, he seems to have realized his error; in later editions of *Birds of America*, he removed the image of the winter hawk but kept the image that had always been labeled as the red-shouldered hawk.

By any name, however, the portrait is another of Audubon's great dramatic images. The hawk has caught a large frog and is carrying it off. The frog's bright green skin and webbed feet are clearly visible. The plumage of the hawk is beautifully portrayed, with a range of tawny hues. The beak is open, and it is easy to imagine that the hawk is letting out a shrill cry. In this side view, a single golden eye can be seen; it is gazing out at the viewer with the intense glare so characteristic of birds of prey. It is unfortunate that the error in identification led to this image being removed from the later editions of *Birds of America*, for it is a fine work of art. Thankfully, however, the original watercolor, as well as many of the early plates, has survived. They clearly show that even when Audubon's skill with identification deserted him, his skills as an artist remained.

CRY OF THE OWL

What kind of bird could make a sound that would startle John James Audubon? The culprit is one of the owls found in Florida: the barred owl. If you have heard its courtship duets, you will understand his reaction. Audubon encountered these owls in the forests of Louisiana, and he wrote with his usual flourishes about how when "the fair moon, empress of the night, rises peacefully on the distant horizon, shooting her silvery rays over the heavens and the earth, moving slowly and majestically along; when the husbandman, just returned to his home, after the labours of the day, is receiving the cheering gratulations of his family, and the wholesome repast is about to be spread out;—it is at this moment, kind reader, that your ear would suddenly be struck by the discordant screams of the Barred Owl." Along with "discordant," he also used the words "strange" and "ludicrous." Although the barred owl's usual call (typically remembered by birdwatchers with the phrase "who cooks for you?") is rhythmic, it is undoubtedly to the courtship vocalizations that Audubon was referring, and they quite justify his description.

Audubon also recalled having the barred owl virtually join him around the campfire at times. The owl was probably attracted by Audubon's campfire menu, which included such entrees as venison and even squirrel. On such occasions, Audubon would sometimes see a barred owl illuminated by the ruddy firelight, eyeing him curiously. "Had it been reasonable to do so, I would gladly have invited him to walk in and join me in my repast, that I might have enjoyed the pleasure of forming a better acquaintance with him." He added with a touch of acerbic humor: "The liveliness of his motions, joined to their oddness, have often made me think that his society would be at least as agreeable as that of many of the buffoons we meet with in the world."

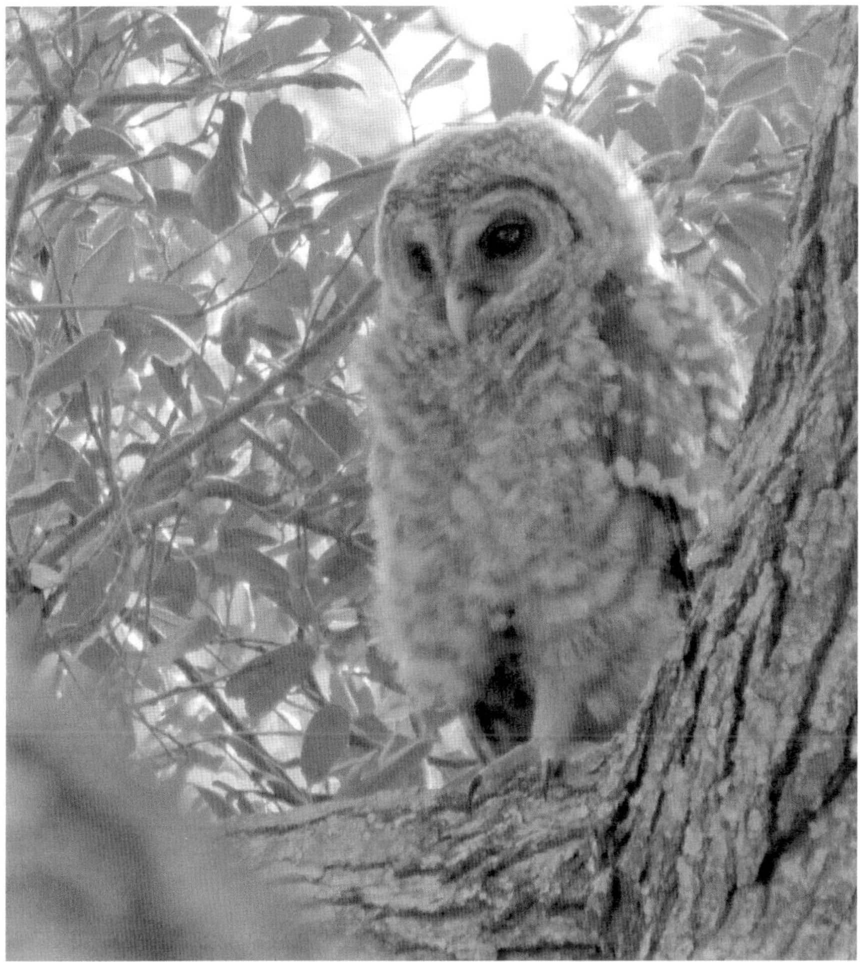

The barred owl is well-camouflaged against the bark of trees, as is evident from this juvenile. *Author's collection.*

For his portrait of the barred owl, Audubon shows it on the branch of a tree, but with its wings outstretched and with an appearance of forward motion. Although it looks like it is about to take flight, it is likely using its talons to walk along the branch, behavior often observed in this species. The color of the eyes is a distinctive feature that Audubon accurately portrays; in contrast to the golden eyes of some owl species, the eyes of the barred owl are dark in color. The painting is very effective in suggesting the softness of the feathers, an important feature in the hunting strategies of all owls. Soft feathers make for nearly silent flight. As Audubon wrote, "So very lightly do

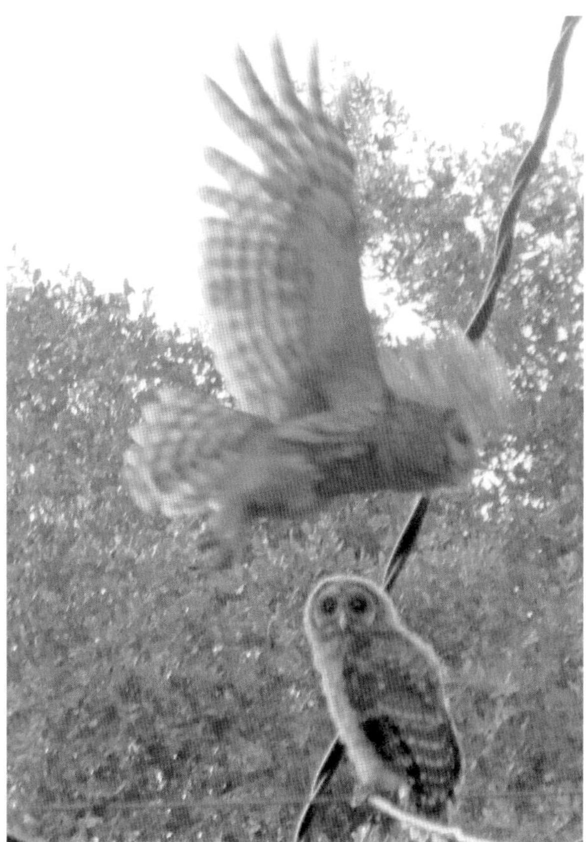

With their soft feathers, barred owls are nearly silent in flight, as Audubon described. *Author's collection.*

they fly, that I have frequently discovered one passing over me, and only a few yards distant, by first seeing its shadow on the ground, during clear moonlight nights, when not the faintest rustling of its wings could be heard." The sense of texture in the portrait of the barred owl is valuable both from the artistic standpoint and from the ornithological standpoint.

Audubon's images of the birds of prey found in Florida are often highly dramatic. They can reflect his theatricality—a trait manifested in both his personality and art. For a certainty, the birds of Florida and the artwork they inspired were treasures that Audubon found in his travels.

15

SANDHILL CRANES AND ROSEATE SPOONBILLS

Birds of America *and the Birds of Florida*

The last few chapters of this book have explored some lesser-known stories of Audubon's expeditions along the St. John's River, in the Keys and to the Dry Tortugas. The story of the success of *Birds of America* is far more famous. The massive Double Elephant Folio and the somewhat less massive Baby Elephant Folio were, and still are, justifiably renowned. Audubon was already a fellow of the Royal Society, and the finished publication brought him further accolades in England and Scotland. On the European continent, Baron Cuvier, a famous natural historian of Audubon's native France, called *Birds of America* "the greatest monument ever raised to ornithology."

The artist himself certainly felt a sense of satisfaction in his work. "The task is accomplished," Audubon wrote. "Few persons can better than myself appreciate the pleasures felt by the weary traveler when he sees before him the place of repose for which he has long been seeking." He then proceeded to imagine such a scene, using it as a metaphor for his own feelings of accomplishment: "He has now reached his home, embraced his family, laid aside his gun and thrown off his knapsack; while his faithful dog, glad too no doubt, lays himself down, wags his tail, and casting glances of friendship around, kindly licks the hands of the children who are now caressing him." It is a heartfelt expression of Audubon's joy at reunions with his wife and family, and at having finished his grand project.

Birds of America was accompanied by a parallel publication that was also of great importance: the *Ornithological Biographies*, a five-volume account of his observations of the birds and his adventures in search of them. Just as he had found a valuable and important colleague in Havell for *Birds of America*, he likewise found an excellent co-author for *Ornithological Biographies*: William MacGillivray. MacGillivray was a Scottish natural historian (as well as an artist in his own right) who had grown up on the windswept isles of the Outer Hebrides, where he acquired a deep love of the natural world. As a young man, he began to study medicine but abandoned it in favor of zoology. By the time Audubon met him, MacGillivray was the curator of the Edinburgh Museum of Natural History. His learned, scholarly nature was an ideal complement for Audubon's adventurous flair; he was Mr. Spock to Audubon's Captain Kirk. It is thanks to their work with *Ornithological Biographies* that we have most of the firsthand observations from Audubon that are quoted in this book.

Following his return to the United States, Audubon settled in New York. He purchased a thirty-acre estate in Manhattan—this was the early nineteenth century, when thirty-acre estates in Manhattan actually existed. Always full of energy, he was soon at work on a new project: *Viviparous Quadrupeds of North America*. (He seems to have forgotten the value of a snappy title.) These images of mammals would never really make the same mark that *Birds of America* had. Today, many people would be surprised to learn that Audubon painted buffalo, prairie dogs and badgers. It is as a great artist of birds that he is remembered.

Of course, he is also remembered as the namesake for the Audubon Society. There is actually no direct connection between John James Audubon and the Audubon Society; the organization was founded late in the nineteenth century by a man named George Bird Grinnell (yes, "Bird" really was his middle name), who in his childhood had been a student of Audubon's wife, Lucy. Grinnell admired Audubon's work, and he felt that the name would be a fitting one for a society dedicated to the study and preservation of birds.

John James Audubon himself died in 1851 at his Manhattan home at the age of sixty-five, having sadly suffered from a stroke and dementia. He had been married to Lucy for forty-two years. "All but the remembrance of his goodness is gone," she wrote after his death. The words are sorrowful, but they testify to a lifetime of loyal love.

We, however, will close our consideration of Audubon, not with his demise but with a look back at two more images from *Birds of America*. These works of art are a fitting conclusion, because they exemplify how the book can still inspire the appreciation of Florida's birds.

"The Colour of the Eyes"

In his observation of the sandhill crane, Audubon made one of his errors. It was the mirror image of the error he had made with the bald eagle and with the red-shouldered hawk. In those cases, he had mistaken a juvenile bird for a separate species. However, in the case of the sandhill crane, he misidentified the species as being the juvenile appearance of the whooping crane.

An error in identification had not prevented him from composing a fine portrait of the red-shouldered hawk, albeit under a different name. Likewise, his misidentification of the sandhill crane did not impede him as an artist. Indeed, his painting of the bird that we recognize today as the sandhill crane is, in many ways, a triumph.

There is much to admire in this portrait—the brilliance of the red crown, the apparent softness of the gray feathers, the distant and ethereal figures of other cranes in the background landscape. Best of all, though, is the brightness in the eye. In considering the varying methods of Mark Catesby and John James Audubon, the words of Joseph Wolf have served as a touchstone: a nature artist who works only from specimens could never "know the true color of the eyes." Audubon's sandhill crane has an eye (singular, since the bird is seen in profile) that seems full of the spark of life. According to Wolf's axiom, this image alone should furnish

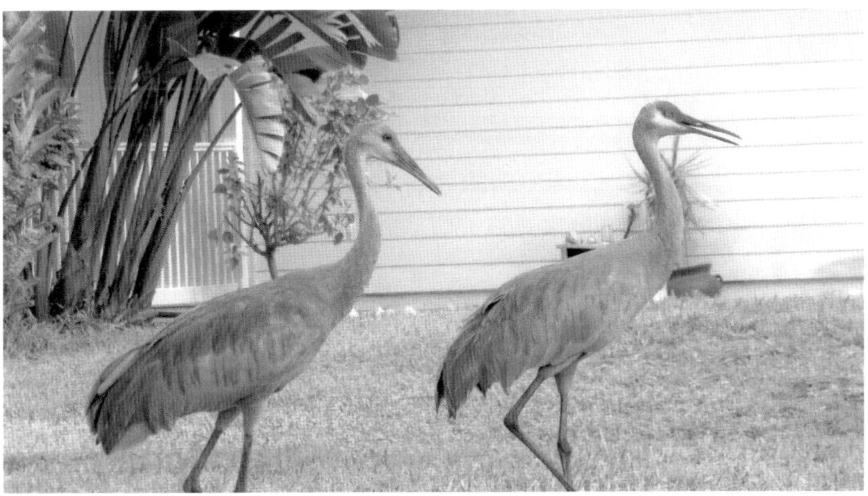

A sandhill crane parent and juvenile. *Author's collection.*

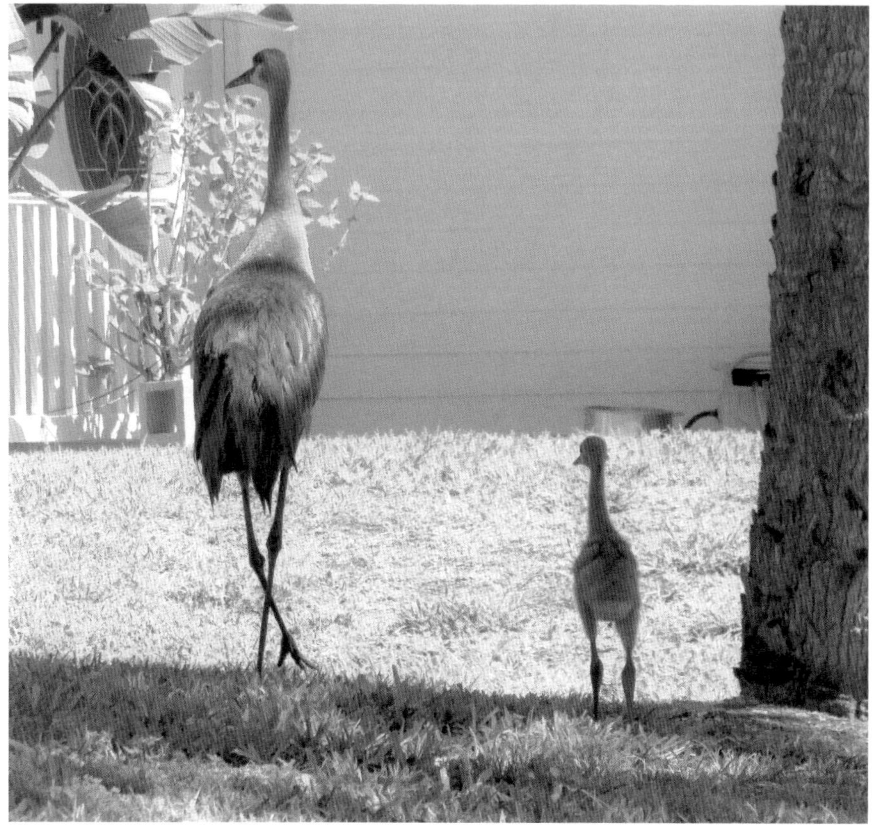

Above: A sandhill crane parent and young one. *Author's collection.*

Opposite: Sandhill crane family camouflaged in a marsh. These loyal birds mate for life and take good care of their young. *Author's collection.*

convincing evidence that, regardless of his use of specimens, Audubon's greatest virtues as an artist of birds came from his observations of them in life. The amber-hued eye of the crane is rich and deep in color, vibrant and joyful in personality. Audubon's portrait of the crane is a beautiful complement to Bartram's sketch of the same bird. It is as if the sketch has been suffused with color while retaining its joyous vivacity.

The distant mountains of the backdrop make it clear that Audubon did not paint the sandhill crane in Florida. Nevertheless, it is a spectacular image of a bird that has a year-round population here. As such, the sandhill crane is emblematic of how *Birds of America* can foster the appreciation of Florida birds.

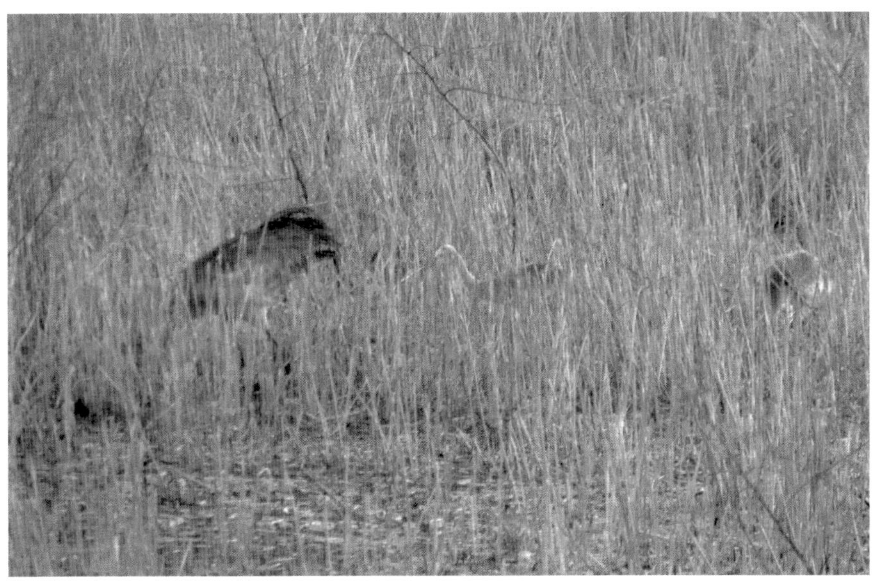

The Color of the Feathers

The tropical and flamboyant roseate spoonbill is a bird that seems distinctively Floridian, and certainly Audubon did see them here (as well as across the Gulf in Texas). His watercolor of this bird leaves the marshy landscape of the background unfinished—it would be completed in London by Havell. Audubon, however, provides a wonderful image of the bird itself. Next to the minimalism of terns and swallow-tailed kites, the roseate spoonbill allowed Audubon to celebrate his love of color. Not only does he convey the extraordinary pink hues of the plumage, but he also shows how the color varies in depth and intensity. And just in case the roseate spoonbill wasn't already flamboyant enough for his taste, he portrays the bird in the full glory of its breeding plumage. Thus, the head (above the marvelously absurd bill) is lime green, and the tail feathers are golden.

"A beautiful and singular bird." Thus did Audubon describe the roseate spoonbill. His portrayal of it with the especially brilliant coloring of its breeding season was not just a fortunate happenstance, for he had observed it at other times as well. He purposefully chose to portray the roseate spoonbill with its brightest glow. As for the expression on the face of the spoonbill, it has been read as anthropomorphic, and to be sure, there is a touch of the humor about it. However, is it really so different from the natural expressions of these birds, which can indeed look whimsical to us? The choice to paint the spoonbill with its brightest plumage was characteristic of Audubon; so, too, is the touch of whimsy. The work of John James Audubon is a tribute to the beautiful, the wonderful, the surprising and the joyful.

Consider this dream that he writes of having had at times while he would sleep in the forests during his travels: "The sky was serene…and thousands of melodious notes from birds all unknown to me urged me to arise and go in pursuit of those beautiful and happy creatures." Suddenly, he would realize that he himself had wings, and he would fly into the sky with the birds that he had been seeking. It was a dream of happiness. And perhaps, Audubon gave that dream a kind of reality with his beloved works of art.

Explorers and Artists

Mark Catesby, William Bartram and John James Audubon were very different in their personalities, their lives and their artistic styles. Catesby was an English country squire and a gentleman of the Royal Society. Bartram was a Pennsylvania Quaker with a gentle and kindly spirit. Audubon was a French émigré with a flair for the dramatic. Yet as different as they were, there were guiding principles that all three cherished. Each one sought to use his art to foster appreciation of nature. Each one wanted to move his audience to look at the beauties of earth and sky with renewed gratitude and appreciation. Each one was animated by a sense of wonder and hoped to spark that wonder in others.

Furthermore, Catesby, Bartram and Audubon were all *observers*—thoughtful and devoted observers. They understood the value of close observation, both in science and art. And they knew that close observation of nature would always be rewarded—with knowledge, insight and joy.

These artists who explored Florida were men of courage and curiosity. They were pioneers willing to face danger in a new frontier. They were adventurers eager to sail to the edge of the map. They were treasure hunters in search of living treasures.

Through their adventures in Florida, through their lives and their work, they were artists and explorers of nature in the New World.

BIBLIOGRAPHY

Mark Catesby

Attenborough, Sir David, Susan Owens, Martin Clayton and Rea Alexandratos. *Amazing Rare Things: The Art of Natural History in the Age of Discovery*. New Haven, CT: Yale University Press, 2007.

British Museum. "Enlightenment." britishmuseum.org/collection/galleries/enlightenment.

Catesby, Mark. *The Natural History of Carolina, Florida, and the Bahama Islands: Containing the Figures of Birds, Beasts, Fishes, Serpents, Insects and Plants: Particularly the Forest-Trees, Shrubs, and Other Plants, not hitherto Described, or very incorrectly figured by Authors. Together with their Descriptions in English and French.* Vol. 1. 1771. http://cdn.lib.unc.edu/dc/catesby.volume1.html.

———. *The Natural History of Carolina, Florida, and the Bahama Islands: Containing the Figures of Birds, Beasts, Fishes, Serpents, Insects and Plants: Particularly the Forest-Trees, Shrubs, and Other Plants, not hitherto Described, or very incorrectly figured by Authors. Together with their Descriptions in English and French.* Vol. 2. 1771. http://cdn.lib.unc.edu/dc/catesby.volume2.html.

———. "Of Birds of Passage." *Philosophical Transactions of the Royal Society* 44, no. 483 (December 31, 1746). https://royalsocietypublishing.org/doi/10.1098/rstl.1746.0078.

Dance, S. Peter. *The Art of Natural History*. London: Cameron Books, 1981.

Durant, Will, and Ariel Durant. "The Scientific Advance." In *The Story of Civilization.* Vol. 9, *The Age of Voltaire.* New York: Simon & Schuster, 1965.

Nelson, E. Charles, and David J. Elliott, eds. *The Curious Mister Catesby*. Athens: Catesby Commemorative Trust, University of Georgia Press, 2015.

Porter, Charlotte M. "Mark Catesby's Audience and Patrons." Florida Museum of Natural History: Artist-Naturalists in Florida. https://www.floridamuseum.ufl.edu/naturalists/catesby.

William Bartram

Ballindaloch Castle. ballindalochcastle.co.uk.

Ballindaloch Highland Estate. ballindalochhighlandestate.co.uk.

Bartram, William. *Travels of William Bartram*. Edited by Mark Van Doren. New York: Dover, 1928.

Bartram's Garden. "History." bartramsgarden.org/about/history.

Bartram Trail Conference. bartramtrail.org.

Castillo de San Marcos. "History and Culture." nps.gov.casa/learn/historyandculture/index.htm.

Covington, James W. *The Seminoles of Florida*. Gainesville: University of Florida Library Press, 2017.

Florida Museum of Natural History. "Artist-Naturalists in Florida: William Bartram." https://www.floridamuseum.ufl.edu/naturalists/bartram.

Gannon, Michael, ed. *The History of Florida*. Gainesville: University Press of Florida, 2013.

Harper, Francis. "Vultur sacra of William Bartram." *The Auk* 53, no. 4 (October 1, 1936): 381–92. https://doi.org/10.2307/4078256.

Harper, Francis, ed. *The Travels of William Bartram: Naturalist's Edition*. Athens: University of Georgia Press, 1998.

King, F. Wayne. "Alligator Behavior: The Accuracy of William Bartram's Observations." George A. Smathers Libraries, University of Florida, 2008.

Paynes Prairie Preserve State Park. floridastateparks.org/parks-and-trails/paynes-prairie-preserve-state-park.

Snyder, F.R., and Joel T. Fry. "Bartram's Painted Vulture: A Bird Deserving Recognition." *Cassinia* 18 (2014).

St. Augustine Historical Society. *The Oldest City: St. Augustine, Saga of Survival*. St. Augustine, FL: St. Augustine Historical Society, 1983.

Tebeau, Charlton W. *A History of Florida*. Coral Gables, FL: University of Miami Press, 1989.

John James Audubon

Alden, Peter, Richard B. Cech, Richard Keen, Amy Leventer, Gil Nelson and Wendy B. Zomlefer. *National Audubon Society Field Guide to Florida*. New York: Knopf, 1998.

Audubon, John James. *The Audubon Reader*. Edited by Richard Rhodes. New York: Everyman's Library, 2006.

———. *Birds of America*. https://www.audubon.org/birds-of-america.

———. *Ornithological Biographies.* Vol. 2. https://www.gutenberg.org/files/57191/57191-h/57191-h.htm.

———. *Writings and Drawings*. Edited by Christoph Irmscher. New York: Library of America, 1999.

Baker, Juanita. *Florida Birds Exposed: Pelican Island Audubon Society Photos of the Month*. Maitland, FL: Abbott, 2019.

Dance, S. Peter. *The Art of Natural History*. London: Cameron Books, 1981.

Florida Museum of Natural History. "Artist-Naturalists in Florida: John James Audubon." https://www.floridamuseum.ufl.edu/naturalists/audubon.

John James Audubon Center at Mill Grove. https://johnjames.audubon.org.

Leonardo da Vinci. *Codex on the Flight of Birds*. Smithsonian National Air and Space Museum. https://airandspace.si.edu/exhibitions/codex.

National Gallery of Art. "John James Audubon: Biography." https://www.nga.gov/collection/artist-info.122.html.

Natural History Museum. "The MacGillivray Drawings Collection: William MacGillivray (1796–1852)." https://www.nhm.ac.uk/discover/macgillivray.

Peterson, Roger Tory, and Virginia Marie Peterson. *Audubon's Birds of America: The Audubon Society Baby Elephant Folio*. New York: Cross River Press, 1981.

ABOUT THE AUTHOR

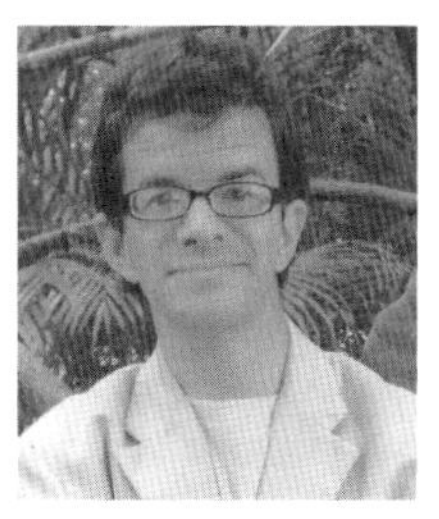

Chris Fasolino lives on Florida's Treasure Coast. He teaches art history at the Vero Beach Museum of Art, and he is a writer for *Vero Beach Magazine*. He has written historical features, travel pieces and serialized mysteries. He has also written a historical adventure novel titled *Men of Promise* about an eighteenth-century voyage of exploration.